MOTOR-HOME GYPSIES:

Practical RV Living Advice & Real World Adventures

Rachel Thompson and Lisa Cross

Motorhome Gypsies is a travel memoir with advice based on personal experience. It is not intended as professional advice or as a definitive guidebook. Please consult with professionals and do your own research when it comes to lifestyle changes, RV mechanical systems, home repair and the legal concerns about where to camp.

Rachel's Email: humanrights4all@aol.com.
RCThom.com or RCThom.net *for her website with info about her books.*

Photographs: Lisa Cross and Rachel Thompson
Cartoons: Rachel C. Thompson
Proofreading: Allison Stein

PARISIANPHOENIX.COM

angel@parisianphoenix.com

parisianphoenixpublishing.substack.com

@parisianphoenixpublishing
/parisan-phoenix-publishing
/parisianphoenixpublishing
@parisianphoenix
/parisianphoenix.bsky.social

parisian phoenix
PUBLISHING

INTRODUCTION:
Ready, Set, Go!

This book chronicles how Lisa Cross and I, Rachel Thompson, traveled the nation living full-time on the road in an RV getting an eyeful and saving money for three years. Here, we share our travels, adventures, frugal ways, and practical advice. This is what we learned living the RV life. If this kind of endeavor is something you want to do, read on, my pioneering friend.

You will notice this is written in one voice, my voice, because two people can't write one sentence. Lisa's influences and words are on every page although it will be me, Rachel, voicing this yarn.

You can't help but notice we are two ladies traveling together. We did have concerns about our safety when we first started out, but being cautious and remaining aware of our surroundings we encountered no reason for alarm. We had few concerns while in campgrounds as most campers are the friendly, helpful type. When we did boondock, we kept safety and self-defense in mind, taking reasonable precautions.

For our own protection and peace of mind, we never waved any kind of flag. It is safe to say that campers are a friendly, talkative community who prefer a non-rocking boat. In most campground and RV park situations, politics and religion are topics which typically drive happy campers from the community campfire back to their own sites. Some places are indeed Christian-orientated — as are the majority of folks in the U.S. — and that didn't matter in our experience. We aren't religious and nobody flashed the evil eye at us. We even spent one winter in Texas surrounded by the faithful without a hitch. Be friendly campers, that is all it takes to keep the peace.

Lisa had retired before we made the leap, with me on disability. This book is not about disabilities, but we have a few words to say about living the RV way with mental and physical health issues.

We embarked on this journey with a limited fixed budget. We falsely expected the RV life to cost all the money we had. We were surprised to find that we saved money every month.

Living the RV way *can* be inexpensive. We quickly became masters of living cheap. Our cost of living was cut in half, which is good, because we needed that saved money for unexpected truck repairs and parts, which *aren't* cheap.

Probably the first question you have is, "Why do this at all?"

Everyone has their reasons. Some dream of a mobile lifestyle, while others are forced into it. Some live the RV life by accident. Perhaps Grandma left a rig to you in the will.

We were dreamers, somewhat well informed, starting under financial stress. How did the dream start for us? We both grew up in camping, hunting, fishing families where we experienced the outdoors resulting in a deep love and respect for nature.

Our goal is to show you the ropes and the possibilities while making your entry into this world smoother with fewer surprises than we had. We learned lessons both the hard and easy way. We experienced way more good stuff than we thought possible, but we also did not anticipate all of our problems and associated costs.

Why we started was one thing. Why we continue is another.

~ Rachel

TABLE OF CONTENTS

SECTION 3: Tips, Tricks, Problems, and Solutions

SECTION 4: Final Considerations

SECTiON ONE:
RESEARCH AND PREPARATION

Buying the First Rig

I'll call any and all recreational vehicles (RVs) the rig. The word rig can mean any vehicle in which you live: Class-C, Class-A, fifth-wheel, pop-up camper, hi-lo camper, travel trailer, bus, converted ambulance, car, pickup truck slide-in camper. Whatever it is, it's a rig for short. Motorhome gypsies don't necessarily live in a motorhome. To us, the rig isn't recreation. It's home

The first rig we bought was a 1978 Dodge Class-C motorhome on a one-ton chassis with dual rear wheels and a 360 motor. We took a long time to find it and spent a lot of time and money getting it ready. It had to be cheap. We only had so much cash and no credit. We aren't the kind to cheat anyone, so finding the right deal was tricky and required patience. We went through that rig tooth and nail before plunking down the cash. And in the end, we missed a lot of issues.

The right rig at the right price is an elusive goal.

We settled on a Class-C for price and emotional reasons. Emotions aren't the best tools for making decisions. The Dodge was held by the parents of a deceased young man who had been fixing it. When we saw it, we made a low-ball offer because of our budget. You have to start somewhere. I didn't expect their reaction. They jumped on our offer of 800 bucks.

We learned before the sale that their son had died. Sad story I won't repeat. The truck had belonged to their kid and these parents were hot to get rid of it. It was a painful memory. They insisted we were helping them. We didn't intend on cheating anyone, but 800 seemed too low. He said after the transaction that they would have taken 100 bucks just to get it gone.

Don't get me wrong, motorhome gypsies thrive on good deals. Low-cost living is our survival art. On the other hand, we are moral beings. We thought we paid too little at 800 bucks and I felt guilty when we got it home.

But, as it turned out, we should have paid $100. A hundred bucks was about what it was worth. Junk yards don't take motorhomes in for scrap: too much waste material and not enough metal. It needed far more work than we expected.

We did all the labor we could to offset costs, but we still needed shop work done. We looked long and hard at the Dodge that day but failed to see it all. The seller didn't have much info to share. They knew nothing about its condition, so in this case, they did not lie. (RV dealers will lie by habit while private owners tend to be honest.) The seller was trustworthy, but he didn't have enough information for us to make the best decision.

Here's a quick overview of what we missed. The overheating issues will be shown later, but the big nut to crack was suspension and tires. Old tires might have good looking tread, but tires are time sensitive and truck tires ain't cheap. We drove it a little before buying but not enough. Had we driven the thing more we might have noticed the front end bouncing (the fix required costly truck shocks with helper springs). We spent $4,000 in shop repairs we didn't expect. The body also had leaks everywhere. Later, we'll show you how to fix them. I had to rebuild all the corners. The cab-over section needed total reconstruction. Simple to do for one familiar with construction, but it took time and money. Of course, we went over the motor and everything attached to it. We did the typical tune-up maintenance stuff any motor needs periodically. After buying, we put about $5,000 into it. Had we bought a rig for that price, we would still have had unseen problems. We knew going in the interior was ugly and we planned to make cosmetic improvements, such as getting rid of the shag carpet. Yes, I said shag and it was orange!

Our philosophy, when it comes to our rig, is to make mechanical systems right for dependability and maintain them correctly. Before we launched, we fixed and improved everything, or so we thought. We tackled the typical stuff old, abused trucks need such as tires, brakes, gas filters, oil filter, air cleaner, tune-up, and suspension work. We even invested in interior remodeling for improved storage, cosmetics, livability, and carry capacity.

Long term the old truck not only paid for itself, but it bought the next rig by way of saving rent money.

No matter how much wisdom, time, energy and money you invest — in the end, expect the unexpected. Never forget that good advice.

We wanted to travel light and compact to cover a lot of ground. The Class-C rig we bought had good space. It wasn't huge, making it easy to drive, and we knew the motor. Older mechanical systems, before pollution controls were a big thing, are simpler, or so we believed, with less electronic gizmos to go wrong. (This later proved incorrect. Basic electrical components can go bad.) Simple means easy to fix, that proved true enough. Later, we'll show you how that simplicity kicked our backside.

In 1978, trucks were not hit as hard as cars were with pollution control device requirements, but all the complexities of an engine remain. Motors aren't simple, but older ones have less add-on junk to go wrong. A crankcase sensor once grounded our car for weeks before we figured out that little cheap part caused sudden stalling. The Class-C didn't have any sensors that could stop the motor from running.

Our initial Class-C rig suited our needs until our needs later grew. In our view, the Class-C was ideal for how we intended to use it. That remained true until priorities changed.

Getting Ready to Launch

"Are you nuts?"

I heard that many times while we prepared to give up our apartment of ten years. We had a nice place in a quaint town. We loved our apartment in that old brick building. The place was close to everything and in a safe neighborhood. Perfect for a couple of middle-aged ladies.

Maybe we were nuts.

We left in a 19-foot, Class-C 1978 Dodge Jamboree motorhome truck with everything we owned in storage or with us.

Who would do that and why?

"Are you nuts?"

No, we were not. Okay, maybe a little.

Turns out, we were ahead of the curve. We saw the RV/van dweller movement coming, and it's still coming. You're reading this because you see it, too.

Make no mistake, there is a lot to consider. We spent a long time thinking, planning and studying before launching, before we made up our minds and committed. (And you should, too!)

Yes, we were nuts but not blind.

We started our journey in 2010. Why?

We suspected that motorhome living was a cheaper, better way to live. We didn't know a lot of details, good or bad, about the full-time RV life. But overall, it was *and is* good and better than apartment or house living in our view. We learned a lot on the road. We didn't plan for an educational experience, but we got one!

Our reasons? Practical and personal.

Life had piled up too high. We were spread thin and involved in too many things, something had to give. Sound familiar? We had to jump off that treadmill. Our initial plan was to take a short trip and test the RV life. Get away from it all for a while. We decided to give ourselves three months and planned to come back and get a new place.

That three-month trip lasted three years and changed everything.

RV Living and Mental Health

One of the reasons I had to get away was due to mounting anxiety. But I was afraid that going on the road would be bad for my mental health. Turns out that was not the case. This book isn't about anxiety but, as it turned out for us, living in the great outdoors where everywhere is home is the antidote for modern pressures.

This lifestyle, we learned, beats back the stresses of life like nothing else. While watching an American bald Eagle take a fish, it's hard to get worked up. When you haven't seen a TV or the Internet in weeks, it takes an effort to feel depressed. In the small city where we lived, the crowds, traffic, noise, sirens, people jostling — and all of that high energy, attention-grabbing — got to us. You don't notice its effects until you live somewhere without it. We were two frogs boiling in modernity's stew pot.

In one way, an RV works like a turtle shell. It grows on you. You grow into it. It protects you and surrounds you with that home-sweet-home, natural security. I always felt at home driving my house-on-wheels.

Because I was. Yeah, traffic sucks but with no place we *had* to be, what's the point of getting bent over it? Plus, there ain't no traffic in the middle of nowhere. Stuck in traffic? No problem. Pull over and make a fresh cup of joe. Take the next exit. It doesn't matter.

For Lisa and I, that feeling of being home offset any worry of the road.

Lost? No problem. In a car, I have panic attacks when lost. That never happened in the rig. For us, driving the RV, our house, doesn't compare to a car when it comes to feeling secure.

Just like turtles, RVs aren't hasty. We drove everywhere slowly. If the faster traffic doesn't like an RV's pace, it can go around. That's what passing lanes are for. When we started on our adventure, we had no idea that driving a house is relaxing. It feels safe. Stress calms down.

Even if you hate driving a car, you might enjoy a rig. A rig floats on the road at its own pace. Even if you can go faster, don't. Driving rigs at higher speeds kills fuel mileage and beats up the rig. Did I mention, driving an unwieldy rig car-fashion ain't safe? Rigs can't stop fast, or steer quickly.

In a hurry? You won't get anywhere but frustrated. So, take a relaxed attitude with you when you go. Sit back and enjoy the ride. Your mental health professional will certainly agree.

Setting Basic Expectations

People do full-time RV living for different reasons. Lots of people make money work-camping. Other people travel for work. RV living lets you go where the work is. We have seen entire families living in RV parks for extended work stays. It's more cost-effective to bring a home with you rather than find and rent one everywhere you go.

Home is where the parking is.

Caveat: There are different kinds of parks from commercial campgrounds to government-owned camps to RV/mobile home parks, which are usually privately owned and mixed-use. In such places, most residences are permanent. Everyone shares the park whether long-term, seasonal, or semi-permanent. We'll share many of our campsite experiences later on.

Parks can be anything from primitive, with no facilities, to luxurious. I use the word "park" as a general term, meaning a paid campground or mixed-use location. Many mixed-use parks take weekend campers.

Keep in mind that even on the road, an income is required. How much money you need depends on your preferences. If you can get by on less and your needs are few, or if you aren't going to drive much, it won't take much money. I have met people living on 1,000 bucks a month. We'll show you many money saving tricks we've learned along the way.

A small budget can work with a realistic attitude and useful aptitudes. We lacked money, but we had skills and the willingness to invest our sweat equity. Life as lower income motorhome gypsies requires being frugal. An awareness of practical considerations and quick-wittedness come in handy.

If you have income limitations, RV living provides lots of bang for your bucks. If we had stayed in an urban environment, Section-8 housing would have been our only choice. With wheels under your house, you have options. If one park doesn't feel right, you don't have to stay.

We started researching RV living a few years in advance. We greatly desired to see more of the country before our finances and increasing age prevented it. We have met tons of full-time RV folks with the same ideas. Some came into the lifestyle with a decent income while many others take the dive with far less money. Money or not we motorhome gypsies are all in the same boat.

This trend is rising: sell the house, get a rig, hit the road.

Why do they do that?

People get tired of the same old life or upon reaching retirement facing an empty nest is too much. Folks get restless. They buy a big-ass, new rig and go to Florida or another temperate, inexpensive area to escape winter. We have noticed in recent years RV parks are filling up after long years of a declining snowbird business. After the 2008 real estate crisis and recession, many seasonal parks took a big hit. People stopped heading south for the winter.

The neighborhood where Lisa and I settled, a traditional mixed park that used to have a 50/50 seasonal to permanent resident ratio, is now filled with novice motorhome dwellers intent on long-term RV living. These new people with new rigs are often clueless and find themselves having problems.

You will avoid many of those newbie issues by reading this book.

Today, our mixed park, and the others I know of in the region, are down to about 10% seasonal campers. It's getting harder to find a cheap seasonal site. Looking back, Lisa and I made the right move. We got ahead of the curve.

One would think the most important part of getting ready to live full-time in an RV is the material preparation. Yeah, it's important. One can anticipate and avoid pitfalls based on foreknowledge. We all do what we can. Mental preparations are also important. One can't foresee the good side of the unexpected, such as the joys and wonders unlooked for you will find.

RV life will expand your world. It takes a lot of nerve to step out of the familiar into a different mode. One should think carefully and plan for it. Being prepared won't dampen the excitement. I can assure you, for Lisa and I, launching into the unknown was a big part of the fun although we ran straight into big problems on day one. It was well worth it. Below, Lisa will give you the lowdown on that.

Lisa on First Launch: Email[1]

Day 1 (Sunday May 2, 2010) Adrenaline:
We were so hyped to be on the road Sunday afternoon that we wound up driving until almost midnight (a 12-hour day).

Turns out we were running a bit hot, and due to concern for the truck, as well as to avoid storms (camping is not much fun in the rain), we changed plans and headed for Rte. 95 South at Richmond. Once we passed Richmond, we hit a truck stop for fuel and some sleep.

Truck stops are an interesting experience, but can be handy. They allowed for a free night's stay, fuel, food, and a dump station to empty RV waste tanks.

Day 2 (Monday, May 3) The nightmare begins:
In the morning, we decided it was time to check our cooling issues. After a bit of scouting and brain-storming, we decided that the abandoned air conditioner condenser coil was blocking the radiator, plus the radiator looked to be fairly clogged. We removed the grill and took out the condenser, finding that the radiator was also partially clogged with bugs, leaves, and road grunge. So that made it easy—all we had to do was wash the radiator off and replace the grill. WRONG!

Being heavier than it looked and having been mounted in such a way as to leave sharp protrusions at its rear, the tight fit of the A/C condenser caused us to slice into our radiator which immediately began pissing that precious bright green "fluid of life," anti-freeze, into the parking lot.

"Yikes! Now we're screwed," I said using many expletives.

---

1 This is an email Lisa wrote to friends and family after our first launch. We had big problems, and in the essay *A Tale of Two Radiators* I'll give more details. This is Lisa's on-the-spot impressions, written when we landed after a harrowing first-day road trip. Later we will share more of our travel log emails.

As I ranted and cursed, Rachel came to the rescue.

"I can fix that! I worked in a radiator shop once. All we need is a torch, solder & flux."

With that list, I took the motorcycle off the trailer and headed to the hardware store while Rachel removed the radiator. Thank Goddess, we had the bike.

Once we repaired the radiator, tested, and reassembled everything, we, being dirty & greasy, sweaty & slimy, headed inside for our first truck stop shower. Best $9.99 I ever spent! Clean, refreshed, and ready to roll, we headed to the highway (now about 3:30 p.m.).

After we had driven a while, it became apparent that we had been successful in our repairs. We stopped at a beautiful rest area, made ourselves a nice dinner, and ate in the picnic area.

Another couple of hours driving and time to fuel up again and switch drivers. As Rachel pulled onto the highway, I heard a sound I did not like.

Upon pulling over to check things, we discovered it was the fanbelt flapping since it was too loose.

"Easy fix," we said to each other.

Wrong.

The bolt that holds the alternator in place when the belt is tensioned was stripped. Deciding that we could do nothing more tonight, we chose to head to another truck stop and hold up until morning. With clear heads, and perhaps some ideas, maybe could get 'something' to fix it.

Day 3 (Tuesday, May 4) Nightmare, part 2:
So, in the daylight things often look better.

Not today!

We tried Sears and Firestone hoping they could use a helicoil[2] to remedy the stripped

---

2 The helicoil is a spring-like device inserted into a stripped-out thread hole. Break a bolt in the engine's block, drill out the bolt, and insert the helicoil. This lets a new bolt gain purchase without the need to re-tap the hole to make new threads. Tapping is how threads are made.

thread issue, but no luck. Not only did they look at me like I was from another planet when I asked about using a helicoil, but they were only part-changers and "not allowed" to do repairs.

Off to the auto parts store, we go. Advanced Auto had a helicoil kit and the required size drill bit, but for the same $40 we were able to get a remanufactured alternator. Only $40?? SOLD!

Once again sweaty and greasy, the truck was again running: belts tight, fan & alternator spinning with no slippage. We washed, got changed, and hit the road (about 1:30). Cut & scraped, burned & bruised, and satisfied with our mechanical prowess, this is when we christened the motorhome "Ruth"[3] to coincide with our realization that everything the previous owner did to this truck was a 'Rube Goldberg' job. The previous owner screwed up more than he fixed, thus the rig is now Ruth Goldberg.

Now we know why there was a box of parts that came with the truck, including fan belts. I sure hope he didn't try to fix anything else.

It is now about 6:30 p.m., and we're a few hundred miles further along. We are sitting in a rest area in Georgia (near Brunswick if you wish to look it up) sipping some delicious homemade coffee. Gosh, it is nice having a kitchen and bathroom with you! But what is even nicer is to have the truck running well with no issues. (Fingers crossed, so far so good.)

The truck ran well, and we made it to about an hour away from Rachel's son, Jason, (near Daytona, Florida) where we ate at Cracker Barrel and spent the night in their parking lot. (They allow RVers to overnight). Nice and

---

3 Rube Goldberg was a cartoonist who drew humorous, elaborate mechanical chain reaction devices whereby one action led to more actions to execute a simple job such as cracking an egg or snuffing a candle.

quiet compared to the truck stop with diesel
engines idling all night.

Day 4 (Wednesday, May 5)

We made it!

We are in a campground in Florida, speaking
with Jason. We will stay in the area for
another day, and then head off to my parents
for the weekend. Hopefully, all will go
smoothly from here.

We will send out another update as soon as
we are able.

~ Lisa[4]

---

4 So how did we get ourselves into that fix to begin with? We bought that rig. It turned
out that Class-C had many more problems and after a few thousand miles, we limped
back to Pennsylvania to deal with them before setting out again. Despite all the problems
the Class-C gave us, that rig saved our lives more than once.

Looking at Used Rigs

You will need a rig. We always buy from private sellers. Rarely have I seen a decent deal at a dealer. Some people have no choice but to buy that way because they need financing. We low-end motorhome gypsies would never finance a rig because we can't. We know some of you can afford it or must do credit because you don't have the cash.

How you pay for your rig is up to you. But we offer this word of caution about dealers.

Dealers don't have your best interest in mind. They will sell you a *look*, a *feeling*, or even a *dream*, but not what you may need. It is good to know what you really need versus what you want before you engage with a dealer. Some dealers are decent people with good intentions, but to be safe, be an informed buyer.

A lot of salespeople don't know much, if anything, about how rigs work. If Mr. Sales Guy knows the technical stuff, he would be crazy to tell you the nasty bits because that info will turn the buyer off.

"Smell? What smell? Don't worry. The shop will flush the tanks for ya."

You'll find out later somebody left a lobster in the refrigerator.

Jokes aside, learning how the rig works is critically important.

Don't get me wrong. It is good to go to dealers and look at rigs for ideas. Knock your socks off. Look at as many rigs as it takes to get the scoop on how they are laid out, what features they have, and what kind of space and floor plans will work for you. Go and gather ideas.

But don't be fooled. Never trust somebody trying to sell you something. The sales pitch isn't gonna give you the low-down. People get starry-eyed and the entire subject of operating your potential new home gets pushed to the back burner and forgotten. If you visit a dealer, make sure they educate you — and please pay attention. Take notes.

For instance, I've heard many stories about how dealers don't tell you much, if anything, about the motor vehicle laws regarding towing. Every state is different. They all have restrictions. Some restrictions are about length, weight, and what type of truck can legally tow what rig. In some states, a 350-size truck (one-ton capacity usually a "dually" with double wheels on the back) *cannot* tow a fifth-wheel type trailer longer than 40 feet and/or so many pounds. Pick-up trucks can only tow up to a certain weight limit. And even in the same class, some 350 trucks have a higher towing capacity than others. If you want a heavy fifth-wheel trailer, you will need the biggest capacity truck. Have you seen the prices of trucks these days?

Before you tow, know what the regulations are and how much weight your truck can tow. That information is usually found on the driver's side door near the hinges. Check with your local Department of Transportation or Department of Motor Vehicles for more details. Make sure the setup is legal in your state of residence. When out of state, if you passed muster at home, the cops aren't likely to check.

This is important: Don't overload the truck or trailer! It's a safety issue. They make regulations for that reason. Stay safe!

With some experience, you get to know rigs by the era they were made. Yes, my 1978 Dodge Jamboree had shag carpeting. RV interior designers mimic current house fashions. So, your rig will have a foothold in whatever era it was built. Whatever is "in" is what they do, then and now. We had orange shag carpeting glued onto the interior motor cover in our Class-C! Most Class-C and Class-A motors are located between the front seats and partly below the floor, unless it's a rear-engine coach. Older vans, like our 1996 Ford Econoline, also use an engine cover but are less intrusive. The point is, if you see ugly decor, look past it. Pretty things are a distraction. Focus on function.

The concept upon construction of these vehicles is to provide a living space just like home but smaller. Designers want to make it feel and look like a regular house. RV interior design is less than ideal because what works in a full-size house won't fit in the compact, mobile space. RV designers sell the illusions of home comforts first with practicality a distant second.

"Look, honey! It's just like home!"

The downside of this is that house features don't work for long-term rig living. If you bring your beloved easy chair, good luck having space for other things. The first thing you will probably do after buying it is to modify your rig's style-space to suit your living needs. A typical rig's cosmetic design may look nice but is not ideal for full-time living. One example we did on all of our rigs was removing the boxed window treatments. They make a rig feel smaller and darker inside. We also either removed or reconfigured the dinette and seating arrangements.

The point is, don't let looks unduly influence decision-making. If you find yourself thinking about how pretty it is, you're getting ready to make an emotional decision. Emotion is not the best way to decide what to buy.

The right space makes your motorhome livable. If you are an occasional camper, any rig can meet your *temporary* needs. My sister had a big fifth-wheel trailer with a bunkhouse so her son could invite his buddies to fun weekend camping trips. That's a good use of such a rig. Towing that pig around the country, however, won't be fun.

By the way, a bunkhouse ain't a house in this case. In the old days, it would be a building like a military barracks. With a rig, the bunkhouse is a small room inside the rig with a bunk bed for kids. If you happen into a rig like that, and don't have kids, remove the bunks and use it for a big closet. More storage space is always good.

Motorhome gypsies going on the road long-term have different needs. Practicality is king. Practical means an investment in your home's livability. So, be aware of your needs — do you hear me? Your needs — versus googly-eyed buying. It's easy to fall for that new car smell only to find out later wet pleather stinks.

Our Class-C had what we *thought* we needed when we started. Over time, our needs evolved and we switched things up. Whatever you buy, you will need to learn how to live with its configuration. You *can* change things, and you *will*. For us, finding the ideal space-use required first experiencing our first rig and later remodeling it. We reworked every rig we have had, and not for looks, but for better organization of the limited space.

When you look at a used rig, think past the surface and consider how to store things. Make sure all systems work and that the roof is good. Understanding the floor plan and how it is laid out matters. If you have a bad hip, are you going to climb up into your Class-C's cab-over bed every night?

No.

Think about how you might change the rig. Think about what you will do, or can do, to make it your own. The 1970s decorations in my Class-C had to go!

As it turned out, changing things for practicality can also improve cosmetics dramatically.

Go figure.

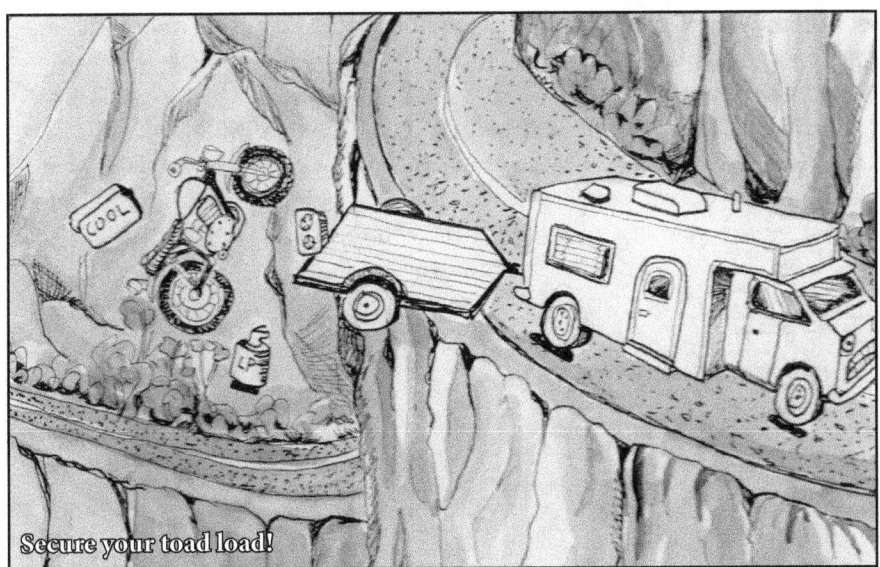

Secure your toad load!

Cheap Toad Haulers-R-Us

Let me talk about our cheap-ass motorcycle trailer and how we did-up that toad-hauler. Toad, you ask? For now, let's just say a toad is any form of transportation you bring along for local use that isn't the rig.

We started in the Class-C towing a six-by-eight trailer for one motorcycle, a generator, and some tools. The bike was the well-respected, lightweight Yamaha TW 200. Dirt bike geeks can tell you all about it. It's great for short trips but terrible on the highway.

What's cool is that the trailer cost us less than 250 bucks, brand-spanking-new with a title.

"What?" you say. "Dang, that's cheap."

We got it at one of the major big box stores, either Lowe's or Tractor Supply, already assembled. Lots of places sell these small utility trailers. Kits were even cheaper. You can still find something similar today, not so cheap, yet still cheap in relative terms.

Ours was so cheap it didn't have a deck, but it did have lights. We attached a four-by-eight sheet of half-inch thick exterior pressure-treated plywood and voila, we had a motorcycle trailer! To that, we added a purpose-built wheel chock and tie-down hardware to secure the bike. We did not cheap-out on the motorcycle chock — because it's critical.

Anything can 'chock' a wheel, which is to say prevent it from rolling. Stick a brick under your rig's tire, and it's chocked. You will need to do that every time you park the rig. Motorhomes have emergency brakes while trailers don't. I only half trust RV emergency breaks. Bricks don't work for motorcycles. Bike-chocks are built specifically to hold the bike upright and in place at rest. You'll still need to tie the bike down.

Later, we progressed to two bikes loaded on that same toad-hauler. No problem. These did not exceed the recommended weight limit. Two small, street-legal dirt bikes served as our toad set for several years. Later, we went to a real motorcycle trailer when we switched to larger middle-weight motorcycles as, again, our needs changed.

After that, we got rid of the motorcycles and went with a car dolly.

By the way, every time we changed equipment, we made money selling the trailers and bikes.

As part of the motorhome gypsy lifestyle, we prefer to buy low and sell higher.

The Differences Between Rig Types

What rig you'll need depends on how little or how much you travel.

What is your objective?

One needs to know what your motorhome gypsy goal is, if you have one, in order to pull it off. What do you imagine the RV life will be like for you?

The possibilities are endless. Maybe you want to meander. Maybe you plan to park and spend long months in the wilderness. Maybe you want to jump-tour, as we did. Maybe you'll go and see as much of this nation as you can. Maybe you're a campground social butterfly or a long-term work camper.

All of it is well and good. But understand — what you need and what you want may not be the same thing.

We had imagined our needs before we launched and picked the rig to match those ambitions. We provided for our concept before launch. To help you determine your wants and needs, we offer some pros and cons of each type of rig that we have used. We researched every rig before buying, but there is nothing like living with it. Plans changed, and so did our rig-needs, which is why we experienced various rig types. Let our experience contribute to your knowledge.

Class-C: When we first started, we wanted the ability to go fast and light with enough capacity for long-term boondocking. The Class-C was the logical choice. Why it was a good pick had a lot to do with being small thus easy to drive. We could get it in and out of tight spots as you will see in our travel logs. It had all the capacities we felt we needed. We planned to do a lot of long-term, off-grid camping. (Long term for us was 14 days, which is the limit of most free federal campsites and the limit of our batteries and tanks.)

And when we say we wanted fast — fast is a relative term. Big, bulbous rigs aren't fast. Our little 19-foot, Class-C was no hotrod either. But it was tidy and compact. Even pulling our motorcycle trailer, we went where big rigs couldn't. Our Class-C rig proved to have serious go-anywhere capabilities, well past what we anticipated, which proved a pleasant revelation. These short trucks, oversquare, with lots of rubber footprints make greater contact with the road surface. Therefore, they are a very stable platform in tough conditions such as snow, sand, and mud. High winds can blow a rig over — but not ours!

Off-road capable vehicles, such as the classic Jeep CJ, are what they call oversquare which means the wheels are in a square pattern rather than rectangular. This makes weight distribution more equal providing better balance, and in turn, improved traction.

Short, Class-C rigs drive like a big van or pickup truck. Class-Cs are typically constructed as a box on top of a one-ton van or pickup chassis. While the steering radius is greater than a van, most people can handle driving a van-based vehicle. Of the drive-it-yourself rigs, the Class-C models are a little harder to handle than driving a Class-B. Bs are less wide than Cs and wider than normal vans, but not bad to drive.

Towing a trailer behind the small but strong Class-C was easy, just as the vehicle itself is relatively easy to drive and park. We also had no worries about height. If you can drive a big-ass van, you won't have a problem with a short Class-C.

The Class-B, by the way, is nothing but a big-ass van with a high top and a lot of utility stuff jammed into it. Older Class-Bs sit on common truck frames, but they are heavy duty using 250 or 350 chassis with van bodies rather than pickup trucks. Newer ones are typically based on a sprinter-style, high-top van. Bs are easier to drive than a Class-C, but they aren't cars and should be driven like one should drive any truck — with caution. Look at any nine-passenger airport van or shuttle. That's the platform.

Class-B rigs are great for short stays but too small for long-term living. They also cost a lot. Not a good value for a true motorhome gypsy. But if you get one cheap or for free, you can make it work. The gas mileage is generally no better than a Class-C. As I keep tabs on the RV markets, I see that older Class-Bs are still way overpriced, and I'll never know why. If you travel alone and often, the Class-B is not a bad way to go.

How Our Class-C Saved the Day.

The C got us out of trouble a bunch of times. For example, we got into a jam once where the Class-C's shortness saved us.

Near the border of Arkansas, the GPS lied to us. More than lying, it tried to get us killed by way of hostile hillbillies. Or at least that is what I imagined as the GPS led us to smaller and smaller roads with fewer and fewer houses until the pavement ended. The dirt road got narrower, fast, and steeper, and there wasn't any light at all for miles. Even the stars weren't out.

What do you do when stuck on the side of a mountain at moonrise? Keep going until the GPS killed us?

The last signs of civilization we saw were more like moonshine shacks than houses. As I drove past the last home before dark, a man sitting on a rickety porch looked at me as if I were driving a flying saucer.

Halfway up a long squiggly hill, it became more than a hill. It became Mt. Disaster. Nothing up ahead but worry. We decided to turn back. One problem. There was no room on the side of that hill to turn towing a motorcycle trailer. Upslope trees, downslope trees, and death if we overran that thin, dirt shoulder.

Back that twitchy little trailer all the way down a mountain? Nope.

No cell signal either.

Yes, the GPS tried to kill us.

Don't worry, we survived.

But it took a couple of hours and a lot of sweat.

We stopped in the middle of the road, chocked the wheels (super important!), and detached the motorbike trailer. Doable, because our toad-hauler was small and light and capable of moving by hand. We would have unloaded everything on it if it came to that, but we managed. The motorcycle had to come off, but that was it. We pushed the toad-hauler offroad just far enough to squeeze the truck past when it was time to hook up.

Next, we did a long, slow K-turn. Inch by inch, we turned the truck around. At times, the back hung over the abyss, but the rear tires remained on solid ground — barely. It took hours to get turned around and hooked up again and out of the woods.

By the time we boondocked later that night, it was past midnight. Small rigs can get into and out of tight spots. Don't try that trick with a Class-A. Consider that the Class-A motorhomes are often the length of a full-sized bus.

There were other times when the small Class-C paid dividends. Like, when we left the flat lowlands near Las Vegas, we climbed into a mountain-range blizzard on Interstate 40 going east. It seemed like a good idea at the time.

Why'd we do that?

A couple at a gas stop had warned us: "There's a storm a-coming, better git over the pass before she blows."

We decided to take a chance and beat the storm. I mean, how bad can it be this late in the spring? Oops. Bad decision.

It was late in the day, and we planned on driving the next few hours to boondock on the other side of the mountain range. That two hours took all night. We got hit with a sudden snowstorm. Not just a few flakes, but a full-on snow squall. Blinding conditions swooped in, and we had no place to pull over because I could not see the side of the road. Interstate 40 was nothing but cliffs on both sides of the road. All I could see driving was a truck's taillights a few yards ahead. I never got the rig going more than 30 miles an hour all night.

It was terrifying. My knuckles have never been that white, before or after. But I learned something about the old Dodge. She was great in the snow. Weight pushing down on big, dual truck tires stuck her to the deck. This truck's ability to plow-on saved us more than a few times. It would go anywhere I pointed it. Stopping, not so much. Truthfully, you don't want to get stuck with a heavy truck. We had jacks on board to get us unstuck, but such an event is never a happy thing.

The Class-C rig's smallness once enticed me to exit the Blue Ridge Parkway in Virginia by way of a steep, twisty, local road. That became a very long short cut. The truck fit just fine, but that decline almost ruined us. The brakes faded badly. We had to pull over, no shoulder again, and chock the wheels with rocks to let the brakes cool. We sat on the side of that road for more than an hour. A local or two stopped to see if we needed help. We managed to make it to flatter grades eventually. We had a lot of weight which taxed the brakes, and the trailer only added mass.

After that, we became very aware of braking capacity. Even with new brake pads, the rig's brakes weren't cutting it. Had our trailer been equipped with brakes, that would have helped. If you tow, make sure your brakes can handle the weight. If not, get a trailer with brakes. (I know it sounds like common sense but don't forget this.) The more weight, the more mass and the less effective your brakes.

Class-C Fast List

Here's a fast list of the good and bad about the Class-C. Keep in mind that Class-C motorhomes come in all sizes from 19 feet, the smallest, to 30 feet, and even longer for the Freightliner-based trucks.

First, the good.
- Easy to drive.
- High ground clearance.
- Lower maximum height than big rigs.
- Sticks to the road.
- Most of them have common gas motors with easy-to-get parts.
- Newer models have slide-outs for extra space.
- Newer models also can get reasonable gas mileage due to computer-controlled fuel systems.
- Floor framing platform is stable, so new replacement floor installations stick well.
- Class-C rigs are easy to do mechanical work on compared to big trucks.

Let me clarify "easy to drive." Easy is a relative term. If you have never driven a truck or van, you may have a bad time until you get used to it. The bigger and longer the Class-C, the more skill it takes to put it where you want it. Just like in high school driver's education, go to a vacant parking lot and practice backing up and pulling it in with accuracy. Do this before hitting the road.

Driving the old Dodge was easy for me because I grew up driving trucks. My dad was a Dodge man. Dodge was known for loosey-goosey steering boxes. I was used to it. Lisa, on the other hand, never felt confident driving the Dodge because of the steering. She was raised on Fords which had tighter steering boxes in the days of our youth. Newer Class-Cs aren't going to have that issue. Nevertheless, drive it before you buy it!

Some down sides:
- Tires cost a lot.
- Changing a flat requires a massive capacity jack, a breaker bar, three men, and a boy.
- If you have to ask about the gas mileage, you can't afford it.
- This is more of a truck than a car, I.E. many costly truck parts. Truck mechanics cost more.

Other Notes

Hauling. The Class-C was indeed good for covering a lot of ground while hauling ass here and there, but there is little room for extra stuff. You can park in many places, camping or boondocking. (Boondocking is camping without campground amenities.)

Outdoor time. The smaller the rig, the more time you will spend outside, which can be good or bad. Portable screen tents and fold-up outside seating are a must unless you enjoy sitting on the ground sharing your meal with ants while being eaten by mosquitoes.
I don't know about you, but if I'm going into the reaches of the great outdoors, I want to be with it, in it, and drink every last drop of it.
Sit inside the rig or bathe yourself in nature? That part is up to you. It does get old hanging out inside a tin can. We think books read better outside.

Toads. You don't have to have a "toad." What's that? It's any small vehicle that is usually *towed* behind and used for hopping around locally. It allows you to go to the store without breaking camp. No need to move the rig.

| **TIP:** We always shop before we stop.

Toads come in all shapes and sizes and we'll show you the motorized options later. For small rigs like our old Class-C, hanging pedal bikes off the back of the rig was our cheap, short-distance toad. Bikes are easy to bring. You can buy bike brackets at any RV store that mount to the rig's ladder. I've seen pedal bikes mounted on the front of motorhomes and towing trucks as well. People even mount mopeds and small motorcycles for local transport on bumpers.

Living conditions. Don't expect luxury unless you go for a big, long rig. In my mind, this defeats the purpose of the Class-C's mobility. Smaller rigs are more versatile, but you sacrifice space and homey features. If going rough is okay with you, and you don't need a lot of stuff, you will be fine in a Class-C. We lived in our tiny one for three years, full-time, without serious complaints.

Minnie Class-Cs. New types of little Class-Cs are popping up in the market now, but they are for people with money. The old, Toyota-based Class-Cs are highly prized by van dwellers and motorhome gypsies alike. They get good gas mileage. Most of them have fiberglass bodies. They are underpowered but crazy dependable. Toyota Class-C rigs (from the 1980s until they stopped making them in the 1990s) are great little rigs, if you can find one. A Toyota is a good rig for one person traveling alone. If you're driving more than sitting, gas mileage is a big consideration. You can't find an older rig that gets better gas mileage than the Toyota. But they ain't cheap. Sometimes, Grandpa has one in the yard and he's got no use for it anymore, and he wants it gone. If that's the case, buy it even if it is not right for you. Clean it up and resell it. Trust me, it won't last.

Looking at Class-A Rigs

Class-A rigs are gas pigs of the lowest order. Once we moved into a Class-A, we were forced to sit more and drive less. Remember, to meet our budget, we had to keep our gas and campsite expenditures equal or less than our previous apartment rent. The Class-A afforded us more comfort and space but less flexibility and less travel.

Class-A rigs are those big-ass, bus-like RVs you see on the road often towing a car behind. They come in all sizes from 24 to 40 feet long. While most of them look like buses, they aren't typically built from buses. Some have front engines running on gas while others have rear motors running on diesel. Some Class-As, like the one Willie Nelson lives in, *are* made from regular bus chassis and drive-trains. They cost upward of a million bucks. Typically, Class-As are built on big truck frames that require truck parts, truck tires, and truck prices. Our A was set up on a P-30 truck frame (think UPS truck). Class-As aren't cheap to buy or maintain. If you get five miles per gallon, count yourself lucky. Compare that to the Class-C range, which is typically eight to ten miles per gallon. Newer Class-Cs might do a little better.

Motor Maintenance: Regardless of whether you have a Class-C or Class-A, they have an engine. Engines must run regularly. Do not park for a year or even six months without running the engine. It's good to run the motor weekly. Take the rig out for a drive at least once every few months, if not more, while sitting. Motor maintenance doesn't stop because you stopped driving.

Also, most Class-As have an on-board generator. Just like with any engine, the same advice applies to generators. Generators must be run occasionally to maintain them properly.

Appearance: While we had discounts for some campgrounds, a few of them would not let us in due to the age and appearance of the rig. Our Class-C *looked* beat-to-hell although it was mechanically sound. Some parks are particular. Our Class-C with all the stuff hanging off it or on it was not an attractive package.

It's harder to tell the age of a Class-A at a glance. Nicer commercial parks are more inclined to let you in if the rig looks decent, even if it is older than their age limit. I've pulled into places with age limits with the A, and our Class-A rig technically didn't qualify to park there. Yet, they let us in without checking the registration because the rig looked good.

Class-A versus Class-C: Size Matters

The Class-A will give you more interior room and storage. Interior layouts are similar in either rig type, but the Class-A usually has more basement storage than the Class-C. Basements are storage compartments under the interior floor level accessible from the outside only. The A gives more usable interior space as well. The driver and passenger seats can be turned around and used as recliners in most units. Some newer C-units can spin the seats, but that's rare in older models.

The cab-over design of most Class-As creates more floor space than a Class-C rig of the same overall length and layout. The cab of the A-unit is much wider. We also used the interior engine cover in the A for temporary storage when parked. It's a handy place to keep the laundry baskets. Class-C engine covers are too small to use this way. Our Class-A had a pull-down bed over the cab's seats, as many will, which we used to store our guitars. Once stowed, they were invisible. This also offered protection from theft — nothing seen, nothing stolen.

The Class-A truck has some restrictions based on its length. Class-As are generally longer than Class-Cs. Many national parks and the like have length limits. Twenty-five feet, overall, is typical. So, if you buy a Class-A, you may not be able to get it into the national park you are dying to visit. When it comes to national parks, size matters. Know before you go what the limits are. Many parks only allow hard-body campers — they don't want campers to become bear food. Pop-up campers are out of luck. You can't camp inside Yellowstone if the camper is too long or lacks hard sides. Between length and height, the A-units don't fit into tight spots.

We rolled into Natural Bridges in Utah driving the Class-C one early season with our choice of sites available, but we were towing so that disqualified us. We were allowed to leave the toad hauler in the station's parking lot. Problem solved. Had we been driving the 27-foot Class-A, we would have been rejected. And extra-rejected since we added a storage box on the rear bumper, making the rig three feet longer.

Class-As limit where you can go. Some are too long and big to fit even in normal campgrounds. They need a lot of room to turn. The newer models often reach the legal road height of 13'-6". Height and length are a problem in the wilder places we favored. You don't want to be caught in tight places. If you get the Class-A stuck, you'll need an army and lots of cash to get it unstuck.

Many commercial campgrounds are well suited for Class-As, because Class-A buying has been a trend for a long time. For motorhome gypsies who primarily plan to use commercial spots, the Class-A will serve well. Many federal and state campsites have made accommodations for Class-A rigs. Touring with a Class-A is possible, but you will be restricted. Some camp spots are simply too small. Maneuvering into tiny campsites is a nightmare. Making a U-turn in a parking lot ain't easy either, especially when towing. (So once again, do your research and practice driving it before you hit the road.)

Driving the Class-A on the road is not bad once you get used to it, but driving it in the woods is another matter. You won't get very far off the grid, so if that is where you want to go, this is not the vehicle for you. While the forest is a difficult terrain for the Class-A, desert landscapes can be reasonably safe for bigger rigs. The Arizona desert around Quartzite, for example, has cheap rate sites throughout the area, such as those run by the Federal Bureau of Land Management. $180 will get you a six-month primitive camping permit there.

Quartzite is a big topic but worth looking into as it's a wildly popular place to winter in. That town goes from a few thousand people in the summer to 1.5 million in the winter. West coast people go to Arizona while north east and north mid-state people go to Florida. We didn't make it to Quartzite yet but we may well try it. From primitive camping on bureau land to commercial campsites, there are a lot of options there. To get a good look at it and see interviews of full-time RV dwellers who winter there with lots of tips, check out the CheapRV Living YouTube channel.

Class-A versus Class-C: Driving

Remember — driving a Class-C doesn't translate into driving a Class-A. You have gone from a truck-like van to a *real truck*, or in some cases, a bus-framed vehicle. Driving a truck, a *real truck,* is nothing like driving a car. There is a whole set of rules and tricks you will need to learn.

Have you ever seen a rented box truck in the fast lane zooming like a race car?

That is a very bad idea.

Trucks don't stop or handle like cars. You must take the time to learn how to drive a truck. YouTube has lots of how-to videos on this. I drove a five-ton dump truck and hauled equipment trailers in my youth, so I had a clue. One thing even a regular renter of box trucks may not know is how to drive a cab-over. Keep in mind — Class-A rigs are cab-over trucks. I have seen the results of bad Class-A drivers' turning mistakes on their scraped bodies and damaged roofs. Driving a cab-over is an acquired skill. One cannot take lightly driving the Class-A.

One of the nice things about driving the Class-A is that they are powerful. They can haul a lot of weight on-board. You can take more of your stuff, but don't get carried away. Overweight trucks are dangerous.

Class-As are also good for hauling toads. I'm sure you have seen one with a car or car trailer hooked to it. Class-As can haul a big toad-load and still stop. But, remember, the longer the rig, the fewer places you can pull over and park. I saw a Class-A jammed under an older gas station's overhead canopy one time. Have you seen low-overhead signs and ignored them? Never ignore them while driving a truck. You must know your rig's height!

Also, while hooked up to a trailer, it is very difficult to reverse in a Class-A even with a backup camera. It is impossible to back up with a car on a car dolly or a tow bar. The shorter the trailer, the harder it will be to back up. Trying to back up a long rig hauling a short trailer is damn near impossible. If you are towing with a Class-A, you'll soon learn to avoid backing up.

One time, on our way out of Pennsylvania with the Class-A, we pulled into a very busy gas station. A local 'Karen' was already there fighting everyone over whose turn it was to get gas. Or maybe somebody cut her off. I don't know. Lot space around the pumps was a madhouse, and I pulled into this storm towing a car dolly.

I inadvertently blocked the entry, and I had to move. So, when the car in front of me left, I moved up. Somehow, the act of my unclogging the parking lot got under Karen's skin. She went off on me like a bottle rocket.

"I can't back up," I told her. "I have a car dolly."

I must have said it a dozen times. It was all I could say.

"I can't back up."

This did not impress her. A cop came and escorted Karen away, as he agreed with me.

I could not back up. Even if I could, a Karen will still be a Karen.

So, what is it like to drive a Class-A? It's like steering a whale. If you are not used to driving a big truck you are not going to like driving the Class-A. For one thing, the Class-C cab is narrow like a van, and you can see the road lines easily. Class-A cabs are eight-feet wide with no hood. That makes it feel odd to drive. You can't see the road or center lines other than ten feet in front of you. It's hard to keep the truck centered. You can't see the road directly below you at all. Lisa hated driving the Class-A. Keeping it in the center of the lane didn't bother me, but other things about driving it did.

Driving a cab-over truck requires a completely different mindset. While driving a cab-over, you must drive past where you think you need to turn before you turn. It's not like a car at all. Where Class-Cs drive like a car in some respects, Class-As drive *nothing like a car*. We can always spot a new Class-A driver. One of the things novices do often is scrape the body. Why? Because turning is a big problem with any big rig when you don't know how. Have I mentioned maneuvering one is even harder while towing?

While you are shopping for a motorhome, I hope you will notice every RV going down the road. Look and see how many have scrapes and dings from clumsy backing up or bad turning. With a Class-A, the top passenger's side rear corner is where they catch signs when they turn wrong. Driving anything long requires the driver to check the mirrors while turning. Car drivers don't have that truck driver's habit, and you will need to develop it. If you go the Class-A route, you will have a different learning curve.

What I hated about driving our 27-foot Mallard Class-A was the squirrelly front end. She lumbered, swayed, and bounced. Steering was okay, but the front suspension sucked. The owner before us had the front end rebuilt which was one of the reasons why we bought it. The work was done, but you'd never know it. Just like the rig before this one, our Class-A had suspension issues, but it wasn't bad enough to justify spending big bucks. At the time, we sat more than we drove, so it was acceptable. By the way, why an RV suspension sucks is because the builders cheap out on suspension parts.

Had we decided to keep that Class-A, and if we had plans to cover a lot of miles, we would have had airbags installed on the front end. Airbags are air-filled, adjustable suspension supplements that work like springs to increase load capacity and improve stability under a load. Springs let the axles go up and down so the vehicle's body remains somewhat level when the road is not. Airbags are your friend, but they can't cure mechanical front-end issues.

Have I mentioned you need to drive it, really drive it, before you buy it?

Back to our Class-A. The big front window was like a glorious fish bowl with a view. Sitting high means you can see far and wide while driving. It also means the sun will cook your brains in no time. Big windows mean big exposure. Ours were tinted, and we had sun shades on the side windows. The front window sun visors were huge, and they needed to be. In a sunny climate, driving the A was like sitting behind a magnifying glass. I imagined a giant kid in the sky frying ants and we were the ants.

"Hey! Lay off, kid!"

TIP: Reflective removable window shades are an absolute must when parked, even if the sun isn't direct. In cold weather, by all means, face that big window into the sun if you can. Your propane tanks will thank you.

Benefits of a Class-A

- Excellent for snowbirds or work campers who take seasonal trips twice a year.
- You can bring a lot of stuff. Newer Class-As have great storage.
- Towing a car or car trailer is commonly done.
- The side wind profile isn't too bad on the older ones like our 1990 Mallard. Have you seen videos of trucks flipped over by high winds going down the highway? I have. Crossing the Midwest or even some deserts, you are open to wicked winds. Most Class-As are too heavy to blow over easily but don't bank on it.

Negatives of the Class-A

- Not great for touring.
- Sucky gas mileage.
- Hard to drive.
- Hard to maneuver, not fun in tight quarters.
- Limited places to park.
- Some parks can't accommodate them.
- If you get stuck, it's gonna cost.
- Because it's a truck, parts and repairs are gonna cost a bunch. A lot of that work would be very difficult to do yourself.
- Changing a tire on the side of the road is not advisable. By the way, you will need to bring along a big-ass floor jack and a big-ass breaker bar in case you have a flat and are forced to change it yourself.
- An RV Roadside Assistance plan may be desirable. Check with your insurance carrier, AAA, and some RV clubs for roadside assistance plans.
- A Class-C can often be repaired at a regular car shop whereas the Class-A will likely require a truck-or RV-specific repair shop.
- These rigs are noisy to drive, unless you have a rear diesel engine.

Types of Class-A Rigs

There are three types of Class-A rigs. Some have front gas-powered engines, like our 27-foot Mallard built on a P-30 truck chassis. What's that? Think of the common delivery box truck you see such as a U-Haul rental box truck or the largest UPS trucks.

The rear engine models are always diesel-powered. These rigs are known as pushers. There are two kinds of pushers. The most common are rear engines used on any kind of truck frame. The other are purpose-built frames and drive trains made exactly the same as a mass transit bus.

Diesel trucks do better on fuel consumption, but diesel costs more than gas. Diesel motors are known for incredible longevity. They are also a lot of money to fix and maintain correctly. Few backyard mechanics have the ability or tools to work on them. They are powerful, so going uphill won't be as taxing as it is with a gas engine. Lisa and I do not suggest getting a pusher for your first rig.

That said, many 350-size pickup trucks, also known as one-ton trucks, have diesel motors. The pros and cons are the same, but because the diesel truck has more torque, we believe the diesel one-ton pickup trucks are a better option than gas powered for fifth-wheel towing.

More about Noise

One time while driving the Class-A, I hit the brakes hard, and the rear locked up. That resulted in a flat spot on a new rear tire. Have I mentioned tires for these things are off-the-charts expensive? I kept the lumpy tire, which added a thump to the other road noises.

Speaking of road noises, you will get that in any truck. Most Class-A rigs have another problem. The motor box is in between the two front seats. That motor box cover makes a nice big place to put things when parked, but remember that the engine is right there. If you have an engine fire, good luck.

I saw a brand-new bus burned to slag. The motor cover gets hot under normal driving conditions, even if it ain't on fire.

When the clutch fan kicked on in our Class-A, you could not hear anything over its noise. That sucker would roar. Adding electric fans and a new oversized radiator did not stop the clutch fan from doing its very noisy thing.

Do you want to hear the radio? Forget about it. Our C-rig was way quieter. The rear motor Class-A pushers are nice and quiet, but the cost of diesel fuel and upkeep isn't so nice.

Fifth-Wheel Rigs

If the Class-A is a barn door going down the road, a fifth-wheel is the whole barn. I haven't pulled one, but I do live in one. Technically speaking fifth-wheels are travel trailers but they don't seem to travel much. Fifth-wheels are great for sitting. Going down the road is not bad. Getting into tight spots is not great. I am told they are easy to tow because they are well-balanced. That seems to be true. They aren't bad to back up and maneuver because the pivot point is located directly over the pickup truck's rear axle.

As for touring, as common sense would dictate, it's not a good idea to drag a big-ass fifth-wheel everywhere you go, but it's not bad to pull a few times a year. Forget about getting good gas mileage. Due to their height, they can't fit everywhere. Many federal campgrounds have that 25-foot limit. You may need to park the rig, park the truck elsewhere, and walk to camp like we did at Natural Bridges Federal Reserve. Between the rig and the truck, that's a long train (but more compact than a Class-A with toad). Very few fifth-wheel rigs are under 25 feet.

You will need a big truck to pull a fifth-wheel. A 350-class truck is the minimum requirement. Not all brands of 350-size trucks are created equal, do your research. They aren't all rated for the same maximum towing capacity. They all suck a lot of fuel. The truck you need to haul a fifth-wheel becomes a very expensive front-side toad. If you want to go sightseeing, it won't be cheap.

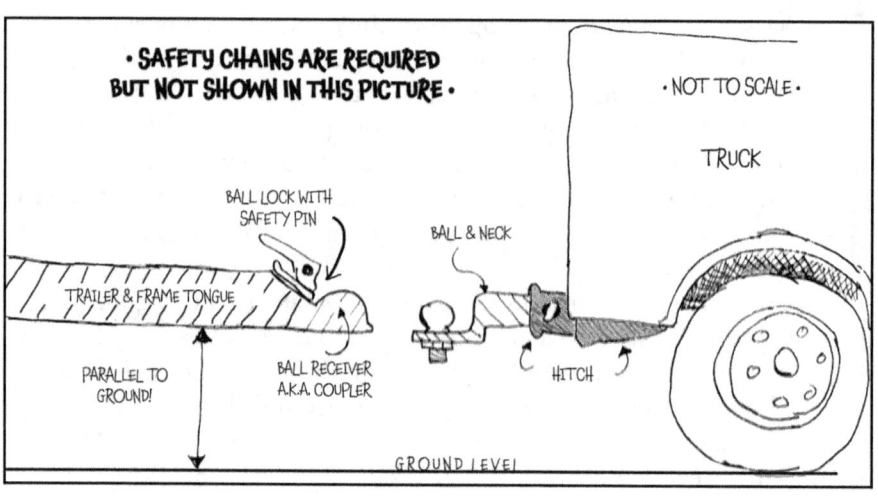

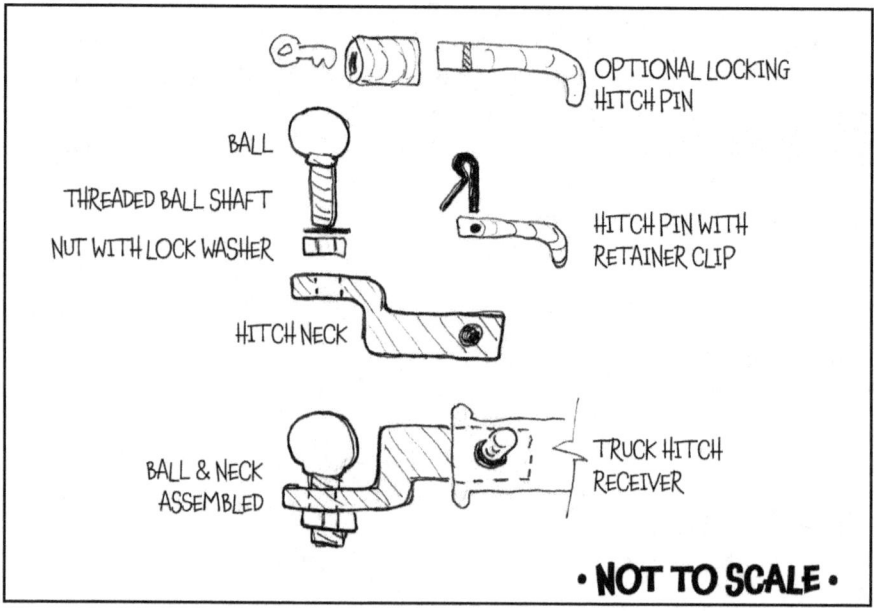

Issues with Fifth Wheels

- Long rigs are a pain to drive in traffic.
- Shopping on your way? Plan on a long walk from the back of the parking lot.
- Off-road, they aren't great.
- They are tall. Don't drive it into the wild woods unaware.
- Because of weight distribution, your truck will get better traction in loose sand or desert climate, but don't count on not getting stuck.
- They are heavy. Our 34-footer weighs 16,000 pounds. That is a lot of mass to stop, even with their brakes.

If you are gonna sit or maybe bounce from campground to campground occasionally, the fifth-wheel may be okay for you. Not a bad snowbird setup, if you plan to park it on-site semi-permanently. For full-time motorhome gypsy life on the go, not so much. If you have a 350-class truck anyway — say you have a farm or a construction business and need that truck otherwise — well, alright then…

It seems to us most of the new campers we meet who bought a fifth-wheel got swayed into it at the dealer. They never thought very hard about what it takes to move one. People with money get them delivered to the snowbird spot, but that doesn't work for people traveling far and wide on a budget.

"Oh, look at that," I imagine them saying when they walk into the living area. "What a nice, big TV!"

Many people leave their fifth-wheel parked in off-season storage. Unfortunately, letting them sit has its own set of problems. Smaller fifth-wheels can be towed with a half-ton pickup truck. These small ones are easier to tour with, but lightweight fifth-wheels are rare to find because they don't make them anymore.

Fifth-wheels are huge with lots of space inside and out. It's bringing a house with you. Fifth-wheels offer a tiny house camping experience. They make a great motorhome gypsy base camp. A lot of the fifth-wheels I see started life as snowbird campers or seasonal family campers, only to wind up a tiny house. But, if you take that fifth-wheel on a six-month sightseeing tour of the United States, you'll need a lot of gas money and you'll be staying mostly at commercial parking lot campgrounds.

Travel Trailers

Travel trailers are what most people think of as a camper. It's an enclosed trailer with utilities which is towed. Technically, fifth-wheels are travel trailers but when we use the term travel trailer, we are speaking of the classic one level camper.

All modern RVs, be them travel trailers or motor coaches, from approximately 16-foot long on and built from the 1970s onward, have commonalities.

What you generally get with every rig type

- A small kitchen with minimal counter-top space: a three-burner liquified petroleum gas stove, an LP gas furnace and water heater, a two- or three-way refrigerator.
- Black and gray water holding tanks, a fresh water holding tank.
- A dinette that folds down for a bed platform.
- Bed platforms with no room for box springs and at odd sizes.
- A fold-out sofa bed.
- A kitchen and bathroom sink, and a shower.
- One or two roof-mounted air conditioning units.
- A low-voltage electrical system with one or more 12-volt batteries which controls or works with the above devices and the interior lights. You also get a 110-volt wiring system just like in any house.

The 12-volt system powers the controllers and serves to let you operate most of the rig's house systems without being plugged into shore power (house current). The point here is that RVs have dual house systems, one for when you are hooked-up and the other for when you aren't. If you buy from a dealer, make them guarantee all the house utility systems, also known as domestic mechanical systems. We'll give you the details on utility systems in section three.

What is *hooking-up*? When you are in a campsite that has hook-ups, that is a place where you tether your rig to a power source that provides house current. You also hook your sewer pipe to an inlet to dump your waste tanks and you get a place to hook your potable water hose into a potable water source. Not every site has full hook-ups available.

Lisa and I have had lots of exposure to travel trailers. They are very popular. You can find them everywhere. The travel trailer is the most common rig you will see. Let's define the term and some general stuff about travel trailers.

What most people think of as a "camper" is the travel trailer. Going down the road, they look like a bus without a motor and the wheels are in the center. The classic type of this configuration goes from very short, at

15-feet long, to as long as 40 feet. The average is between 27 and 32 feet. They are no more than 102-inches wide while being towed. That's the maximum width allowed on United States highways.

The front-toad truck will need extended mirrors to tow a travel trailer. Many newer trucks, especially those with a tow package, have them already. If not, aftermarket mirrors can be added.

Travel trailers date to the 1920s. After World War II, an interest in camping and touring the nation exploded and manufacturers reacted to the demand. The most recognizable of these travel trailers from this era were the Airstream, still in business today. Airstream traces its roots to the wartime aircraft construction industry. Post-war aluminum sheets used for skins on aircraft bodies and lightweight aluminum structural parts had no place to go once hostilities ended.

Airstream took advantage of these left-over materials and built these campers in the same way as an aircraft fuselage but mounted it on a steel, road-going frame. The exteriors are all aluminum and polished shiny. The front and rear end are rounded off like the nose of a bomber. They look the same today as they did when they were first invented. Airstreams are the most expensive travel trailers on the market. They pull nice. The smallest model currently is the pup at 26 feet.

The Argosy brand is very similar in construction style and function but a little less money. Airstream and Argosy tend to be owned by people with money to burn. They are nice, and they are tougher than the rest, but you pay for that. They also do not have a feature called a slide-out.

A slide-out is a section of an RVs body that extends out from the main body while parked, giving the interior more floor space. Slide-outs must be pulled inside the body to go down the road. Any RV can have a slide-out, be it a Class-A, Class-C, travel trailer, pick-up truck camper (the kind put into a pickup truck bed), and even pop-up campers.

Slide-outs were not universally used until the mid-90s. Many new small rigs will lack them. Our 1990 Mallard, 2000 Sunline, and 1978 Class-C Jamboree did not have slides. Airstream and Argosy do not use slide-outs so their floor space is static.

Vintage and antique campers are popular projects for hobbyists. Vintage Airstreams are very expensive and even a junk pile version of one cost a pretty penny. The other popular campers for restoration are anything old but the ones called "canned hams" are very short and were built from the 1950s into the early 70s. These campers are too small and do not have the modern amenities a long-term camper needs. Not a good choice for a motorhome gypsy going full-time. These are nice, fun rigs for weekend camping trips.

The smallest camper of all is the teardrop trailer, used from the 1930s through today. Again, hobbyists often build their own teardrop campers. The plus side of the tiny campers is they can be pulled with a car. Typically, many of the smaller trailers, new or old, don't have their own brakes! They are light, but remember — any extra mass means longer stopping distances, so don't overload them! Stay within the car's maximum weight capacity.

Why We Bought a Sunline Travel Trailer

How long of a rig you need will depend on what you need to do with it.

Here, we'll talk about our Sunline model 19T and why it is perfect for how we use it. The overall length of the Sunline is 19-feet 5-inches with a living space inside of 17 feet long by 8 feet wide. It's our current rig for making tracks. We could live in it if needs be. This is a good setup for motorhome gypsies who wish to cover a lot of ground.

Why this rig?

Here is our reasoning.

The Sunline is:

- Small enough and light enough to tow with our E150 van. An oversized truck isn't necessary. That's generally true for lightweight travel trailers. The bigger and longer the travel trailer, the more power you will need. (Stabilizer bars, an extra expense, help larger units pull straighter and with less sway. A small trailer doesn't usually need stabilizer bars.)
- Small enough to go almost anywhere, yet large enough for comfort.
- Not too cramped and is well equipped. It's not too cramped.
- Able to be pulled by the car, which provides more storage inside the van.
- On two axles with brakes for balance and safety.

Because of the dual-axles, she is heavy for a small rig and close to the maximum towing capacity of our van, which we don't like. Lightweight travel trailers are usually single-axle, which can be an issue during a blown tire. Single-axle trailers jackknife easier, which is why we wanted a double-axle rig. If we blow out one of the four tires, it's not a big deal. I've seen single-axle trailers go sideways and drag the tow vehicle off the highway. I once saw a Jeep towing a boat on the Garden State Parkway in New Jersey do that. After the blow out, the trailer swayed wildly. When the driver caught on, he hit the brakes hard, causing the jackknife.

> **TIP:** If the trailer sways, don't pull off suddenly. Take your foot off the gas and glide down to a lower speed until pulling over is possible. Don't panic and hit the brakes! Our primary use for our Sunline is for no-hotels traveling and short adventure trips. Short trips require less interior space than long-term living. It also serves as a base camp for hiking, sightseeing, etc., while traveling. Small travel trailers can work well for motorhome gypsies on the road full-time. This small rig has more usable space than our Class-C of the same size had.

Driving and Towing

I'll mention more about jackknifing—when your truck is going straight down the road and your trailer isn't, you're going to have a bad time. How's that happen? The trailer sways so much it goes sideways, which can make you lose control of the vehicle you are driving. This goes for any kind of trailer. To minimize the risk of jackknifing, make sure the load of your travel trailer is balanced.

Balancing? How?

The load you store inside or on the trailer should be spread equally so that there is no concentration of weight in any one location. Campers are designed to be balanced and should go straight while towing when the waste tanks and water tank are full. Too much weight in the trailer's front will tax the tow truck's suspension, making steering less responsive. It's not good for the truck, either.

Too much weight in that back of the trailer takes pressure off the hitch and lifts the truck's back-end, making steering too light and less effective. Either way, an unbalanced load promotes swaying and that can cause jackknifing.

Tongue weight is important. Every trailer has a tongue weight preference which will be listed in the maker's specs or stamped on the trailer frame near the hitch ball receiver. The tongue is the trailer's frame that protrudes forward past the body. It's A-shaped. Tongue weight is the amount of down-force pressure put on the hitch of the towing truck. This force should not tax the truck's suspension. When a trailer is hooked up to a truck hitch, the tongue frame should be level to the road and the truck hitch. The truck should sit about as level as normal.

How do you know you have the correct tongue weight?

Tongue weight should be 10- to 15-percent of the trailer's overall weight. Too much or too little will cause the trailer to act badly. Too light is worse than too heavy, but neither is good.

If you plan to tow, and never have before, you need to know a few more things.

Not every truck is set up to tow. Pickup trucks, be it the 150, 250, or 350 size, often come with a tow package. That means the truck will be equipped from the factory with higher capacity, heavy-duty suspension and a tow hitch. Sometimes better gearing for towing is provided in the axle or transmission, and sometimes a bigger-sized motor is used. There are variations above stock equipment for improved towing.

What all tow package trucks have in common is the wiring necessary to hook the truck lights to the trailer so that the trailer has normal vehicle lights. This wiring can be added to any truck or car. The other thing that tow package trucks have is a hitch consisting of a hitch frame bolted hard to the truck with a receiver hole. The neck and ball that slides into the square receiver hole isn't usually provided.

The hitch receiver is where you stick the neck and ball which is held in place by a locking pin. The neck and ball are removable. Balls come in several sizes and the trailer's tongue should have a stamp telling you what size ball is required. The neck can be had in many different height offsets. This is how one hooks up level. If the neck and ball are too low or high, one can change the height by way of offset necks or a multi-height neck.

Balls and necks are commonly found in any auto parts store, camping stores, and places like Tractor Supply. Necks are adjustable because the trailer's frame should be level when hooked up and the truck's hitch receiver height is usually different than the trailer's ball receiver.

One more thing necessary for towing is a brake controller if the trailer has brakes. Tow-package trucks always have the wiring you need, and a controller, but older trucks almost never come with a brake controller. If your trailer has brakes, and we mightily recommend that it should, you will need the controller. This electronic device operates the trailer's brakes and coordinates how the truck and trailer's brakes work together. This is something best installed by a professional.

A controller has a slide switch on it so one can engage the trailer brakes while driving without using the truck's brakes. Why is that good? We always test the trailer's brakes before shoving off. I roll down a dirt road slowly while Lisa watches. I engage the trailer's brakes only. The trailer's wheels skid. Brakes work!

The other thing is when and if the trailer starts wagging, a little blip on the trailer brakes may stop it. I've been told about this anti-wag method, but I never tried it.

Anyway, the point is if you are shopping for a truck, get one with a tow-package as that will save you time and money.

The other thing you need to know about towing a trailer is backing one up is no picnic. Again, this is something you should practice if you haven't done it before.

To conclude, in general, travel trailers are a good option if you will sit more than drive. They are great for weekend getaways. A lot of people live in them full-time but most of those don't go touring. If you want to make tracks and see the nation, the small travel trailer isn't bad. Leave the 30-footer home.

Setting Up and Setting Out

This is how we set up our first rig:

We used the cab-over bed on the Class-C (and later our Class-A) as storage for our guitars and other effects. We had to bring our guitars, of course! What's a campfire without singalongs? We organized clothing inside easy-to-move containers. Instead of the cab-over bed, we used the fold-out sofa and fold-down dinette as the platform for our airbeds.

We opted to inflate and deflate our beds every day to supplement the inadequate cushions. One must have a good bed no matter where one sleeps. If an airbed is something you might consider for your comfort, do not buy the common, off-the-shelf ones. They won't last. We always had spare mattresses with us until we found a company that makes hospital-grade airbeds. Then, we recycled our busted K-mart beds by cutting them up to use for tire covers.

The former owner had built an eight-by-three-by-three-foot storage box onto the rear of our C-rig. We liked it so much that we later installed a plastic pool box about the same size onto the back of our Class-A rig. If you're thinking you'll need more storage, there's always the roof. When living full-time in the rig, there is no such thing as "extra" storage. You need every pocket you can get. Our Class-C had a tiny shower, and it worked, but we used it more for storage than for bathing. We relied on campground and truck stop showers frequently.

We already talked about our toad trailer which we loaded with small street-legal dirt bikes, a generator, (which we never used and later sold.), solar panels, tools, and spare parts. We always needed spare parts. We had, but didn't need, water cans. It turns out we needed gas cans and spare LP tanks which we didn't pack setting out.

The outdoor living gear we loaded included an all-band radio, a portable grill, which worked great, extra grill-size one pound propane tanks, outdoor campfire grates for cooking and a basket device for cooking fish or veggies on an open fire. We stored the outdoor fold-up table and chairs on top of the rig's exterior storage box.

And the interior? We had remodeled the C-rig, but didn't do anything radical with space. On the C, we added an extra battery, a smart charger, and some wiring to hook up solar panels, along with the mechanical work already mentioned. We did go radical fixing up the Class-A, fifth-wheel and Sunline's interiors.

Smart chargers and battery isolators are built into modern rigs. The isolator lets the truck alternator charge the trailer's house batteries while driving without drawing down the truck's battery. It's a standard feature on any late model motorhome. Smart chargers prevent the house batteries from being overcharged and boiling off their electrolyte. We added one to the C-rig.

We had successfully packed for all weather and off-grid. One early adventure radiator mishap would have been worse if had we not been ready to deal with mechanical problems. Before you start out, think things through. Pack logically.

Lisa and I have the mechanical abilities to deal with most issues that can arise in an RV. Lisa taught industrial arts and engineering and worked in industry. I worked in a radiator shop in my teens and as a construction professional for 25 years. Between Lisa and me, we could fix most problems. Important to bring along is repair skills.

If you want to live the motorhome gypsy lifestyle, you should know how to fix things or have the financial resources to pay someone. But be cautious — having others fix your rig might bankrupt you. If you have neither skills nor resources, I'd recommend sticking to a travel trailer and truck versus a full-fledged, self-contained motorhome.

I know we mentioned this when we discussed selecting your rig, but it's worth repeating. Any shop can fix small trucks. Big motorhomes based on commercial trucks create complexities and double the cost of mechanical repairs. Any RV, new or old, is essentially a handyman special. RVs require tinkering and attention. If you stay in an RV park long-term, there will be people to help you. Most parks know or even have a handyman who works reasonably cheap.

Camping people are generally nice folks willing to lend a hand. In the park where we live, any time someone has a project to do, such as, build a shed or set up a canopy, everyone in sight will ask if they can help.

When we set out, we had high hopes and our best preparations. It worked out. Yeah, we had a few surprises. We handled these by loading a positive attitude combined with the confidence we had earned by working on our rigs ourselves. We knew her well. Get intimate with the rig before you launch.

Everything seemed good, but sometimes, it doesn't stay that way.

Before You Go: Think about Mail

Most of us full-timers have what we call a home base which is a place to pick up the mail, launch from and return to in time of need. In our first years we didn't have a fixed, permanent landing spot but we had options for temporary bases. In our case, home-base was wherever we wintered or summered and sometimes it was our old home grounds for a long stay. Home base changed location as our needs changed.

Wherever we were we considered it home, yet we always had a place to go if we needed medical help from our old providers or a fresh start. We also returned to a home base whenever we needed to make big repairs. For example, when we needed major do-it-ourselves mechanical repairs on the Class-A (which we will say more about later), we went to my sister's house in N.J. We didn't need to pay rent, which helped pay for parts, and we had room to work.

New Jersey was home base for two months one summer. That said, home base also has a mundane but important function: That's how you get snail mail like vehicle registration. One needs an address even if you never go there. RVers often call the legal address home base.

In the beginning, we had a friend who lent us an address. This provided a legal residence so we could register our rig and get mail. That friend would forward our mail to wherever our current location was. When we summered there, we paid money or earned our keep by doing jobs she needed.

Motorhome gypsies are frugal so having a friend do our mail was a bargain compared to forwarding services. Look into this online to find the right state to be your home base for legal vehicle registration. You need to have an address, but you don't need to live there. One can establish an address in some states at a mail forwarding service without needing to be there much, if at all, such as in Florida and the Dakotas.

Persons who travel will do well by making a mailing service your home base address. You will need to plan a longer stay somewhere and coordinate with the service to receive delivery. There are fees to register, hold and ship your mail but it's a relatively cheap way to ensure receiving mail and legal status. Friends and families aren't always prompt in getting mail to you. The big bonus is when you do get mail, it's like Christmas, except for the bills, of course. These days, bills get paid online so the mail aspect is less important. However, that legal address is all important which is what makes the full-time motorhome life possible. Home may be where the heart is, or where you park, but home base is where your legal residence is!

Septic Tanks: Oh Poop!

Let us get it over with.

This is the most important thing you need to know about RVs, and it ain't pretty.

Unfortunately, if you are going to travel or live in any kind of RV, you will need to deal with poop. Specifically, your waste tanks. There is an inescapable need to actively manage everything in your RV from the living space to house systems. All of this must be understood enough to deal with problems.

This is a known unknown.

You will have big poop problems, unless you heed this warning.

Poop problems?

I know you aren't interested in waste tanks, but let me show you what happens when you don't pay attention to them. Our neighbor Pat, who has since moved on, had a late-model, low-mileage, Class-C in good condition and worth about $12,000 at the time. She had to sell it and only got a few thousand for it. In part, she got a low price because she didn't ever run the motor, and motor-related rubber parts go bad (such as seals and gaskets). The gas tanks were full of rusting crud. The fuel filters were clogged with old gas. The tires were cracked. Had she driven it regularly, none of that would be a problem except the tires aging out. The truck was in fair repairable condition other than *one thing*. The black tank was clogged solid. The gray water tank wasn't good, either.

Bad waste tanks were the deal breaker. Motors can be fixed, but the waste tanks...They had to be removed and replaced. With that Class-C's body panels, there was no way to replace them without hacking up the body.

Once sludge forms and hardens, it is dang near impossible to remove it.

Why?

Improper holding tank care and the nature of how these tanks work is the culprit. For now, I'm talking about black water tanks, that's where the poop goes. Gray water tanks are where the used sink and shower water go.

Because Pat didn't know what you are about to learn, she ruined her camper.

Waste tanks must be maintained. Black water tank care is paramount.

I would have bought Pat's rig, but those tanks scared me off. The way they were installed made the problem far too costly to fix.

The rig had sat for years. Therefore, it needed everything a sitting rig needs.

It looked great outside, and the inside wasn't bad — barring some cat hair — but the work and money involved to repair it didn't make sense. If the tanks were serviceable or possible to replace without major surgery, that truck would have been worth bringing back to life.

Black water waste tanks are the number one common problem for new RVers. So, before we get into some personal experience storytelling, let me explain what you need to know about and do for your waste tanks.

Standard waste tanks on an RV are designed for *temporary* holding in a moving vehicle. When a rig drives from location to location, it rolls the liquid in the waste tanks, loosening most of the stuck, nasty bits. The waste tanks clean themselves, to a point. If you drive frequently, especially in comparison to how much you use the toilet, your well-traveled RV will have clearer waste tanks. The more RVs sit, especially with people inside, the more sludge will stick and build up on the interior of the waste tanks. It's basic physics. That poop dries over time creating fecal matter cement.

I see this all the time. A person buys a rig and finds the waste tanks half-full of poop cement. Often, the buyer and or the seller don't know any better. My snowbird friends who bought a used fifth-wheel learned the hard way. They used the bathroom as they would in a house for a couple of seasons. Any rig that sits for more than a few weeks will develop sludge on the bottom of the tanks. Tanks are vented so they do dry out. This fifth-wheel sat for more than one winter, so you can imagine the problem!

Don't try this at home! My friends used muriatic acid and days of snaking to clear the tanks. It's a trick I considered with my friend Pat's rig, but in the end, I thought breathing acid fumes proved too risky. The regular, house-style plumber's snake designed for household drains couldn't do the job. Eventually, they cleared the tank, but it took days of effort. What a mess!

Salesmen will tell you that your rig has a black tank cleaning system with "spray action." My experience, and the Internet agrees with me, is that these spray systems don't work. These systems aren't designed to prevent the waste issues of a sitting rig. I've seen video demonstrations using clear plastic tanks to illustrate how spray system's lack of utility.

What I recommend — and it works better than a sprayer — is an intentional sloshing of the black water tank on the regular while driving the rig.

Here is something you can do every time you move the rig:

1. Start by dumping the tanks before you leave camp.
2. Fill them one-third of the way with a mix of water, dish soap, and RV tank deodorant. (Available at camping stores, Walmart, or anywhere camping gear is sold).

3. Finally, drive. Do this every time you take the rig to a new site, and the tanks will be sludge-free — as long as you go place-to-place fairly often.
4. Here's a trick for you. Put a bag of ice cubes down the toilet with a ⅓ full tank of fresh water when you drive out. Ice knocking around helps clean your tank.

If your rig sits a lot, there is no way around it. You will get sludge. You will need to deal with it.

How best to deal with it?

Regular and effective sewer jetting worked for me. Jetting is no joke. This works best when the toilet is located directly over the black water tank so you can direct high-pressure spray from a special jetting wand attached to a garden hose effectively.

This device narrows the water stream to create pressure. This process is what built-in spray systems are supposed to do, but don't do very well. The built-in spray system can't push enough direct pressure at the trouble spots. You need almost as much power as a power-washer. Don't use a power washer, it will be a disaster. Too much power may puncture the tank.

Be warned, during this process, poopy water will splash. Stuff rags around the toilet hole to minimize the mess as you use the wand.

RV toilets are not like house toilets. There is no trap built in. RV toilets hook directly to the three-inch waste pipe. If your waste pipe takes a bend when you look down the hole, a wand or jetter stick can't work.

You need something similar to what every town with sewer pipes, storm drains, and processing plants have — a flexible sewer-jetter. The commercial jetter is a huge truck. You don't need that much power, but the concept remains true.

I made a simple jetter. I used brass gas pipe fittings by way of reducer fittings, allowing a larger-size part to fit into a smaller size. From the 5/8-inch hose thread to a quarter-inch short pipe took three transition parts. My jetter when assembled was about six inches long and could make a 90 degree turn inside the three-inch sewer pipe.

Any common garden hose can be made into a jetter. Hardware stores have a brass fitting section. Brass fittings come in all sizes and reducer combinations. You can combine brass gas pipe reducing fittings, which are transitional connectors and fit them to a garden hose until you get to a quarter-inch nozzle. I like to use a four-inch-long, quarter-inch threaded brass pipe on the end. The idea is to force the water through a narrow opening.

Once again, **YOU MUST** make sure the tanks are clear before you buy any RV. If you can't see down the hole, it will be hard to know the condition. The smell test won't tell you everything. Many RVs come with electric tank monitors that are supposed to show the tank's level, but even if they are accurate (and they often aren't), they don't show you sludge buildup. Don't trust the monitor.

You can ask the seller and hope for the best. You can buy it under a contract stipulation that the black tank is clear.

If you can hook a flow gauge onto your dump valve or exit hose, flood the tank and then dump it to measure how much water was held. If the tank is supposed to hold a certain amount, (your rig's paperwork will tell you) and it doesn't expel the amount of water it should, you have sludge. Something is occupying that space and it ain't pretty.

Most rig waste tanks are mounted below the frame and are spread out wide and flat to distribute weight. Tanks vary in height between ten inches to about fifteen inches. If you look down the hole and *can* see sludge, one way to know how thick it is, is to poke a stick in there. Then, look at the stick. Use it like a dipstick on a car that checks oil level. If the dipstick sinks more than a ¼ inch you are gonna have a bad time.

The best tank situation, and something to look for before you purchase, is not only clean but *accessible*. The best tanks are the ones directly under the toilet *and removable*. In some rigs, the waste tanks cannot be removed. These tanks can't be cleaned well. Even if you drive often, you will still need to jet clean the black tank occasionally.

The way tanks work is you keep them closed so water and materials are held in place until the tank is full. You then dump the tanks and the pressure of the water weight accumulated inside the tank pushes out the refuse. You keep your tanks closed by way of the inline dump valves.

A lot of tanks are made too light and thus weak. They are typically made from ABS (Acrylonitrile Butadiene Styrene) plastic and while ABS is strong, manufacturers make the waste tanks with the thinnest plastic they can. They will say it's for weight savings, but what good is that when the tank breaks due to overloading or gets a hole when a rock from the road hits it.

Tanks do break, and leak at times, and they may need to be replaced. While still in the shopping phases of deciding on a rig, it is important to check that the tanks are easy to access and able to be replaced. Make sure you see this for yourself, don't take the word of a salesman without evidence. And remember — the ideal position of a black water waste tank is directly under the toilet with no bend in the waste pipe.

Welcome to My Personal Poop Nightmare

I think every motorhome gypsy has had a poop nightmare to share and here's mine. Our black water tank started leaking in our home base Carriage brand fifth-wheel rig. We had been sitting, relying on the on-board spray system for regular flushing and maintenance. As I warned earlier, it didn't work, but I didn't know it at the time. Sludge had built up and added weight to the system. The extra weight caused the tank to crack at the seam in the top-mounting flange.

I had to remove the tank to fix it, but before I could remove it, it had to be cleaned. To get at the sludge, I removed an interior basement wall, cut the three-inch PVC waste line pipe, and installed a two-to-three-inch T-Y fitting to get my jetter where it needed to be. I also added a short two-inch pipe with a removable cap for repeated access.

Good thing I know plumbing!

It took hours of jetting to clear the dense, heavy sludge build-up. I also discovered that the tank was suspended on rails from the top flange with no support under it — a poor design!

After jetting, we took our tank out. We patched and reinforced where the ABS plastic tank had separated from the ABS mounting flange. Once I fixed it using ground ABS and glue, we returned it to its place, suspended from that crappy flange. I didn't like it. I designed a system to support the tanks from the bottom. It took me at least three days to create and install a way to hold the weight of the tank.

Two months later, the tank's flange cracked again. It sludged up again despite my jetting it about every two to three weeks. I should have done it every few days. I took the tank out again. I discovered a different crack, fixed that one, and put the system back together. In no time at all, the tank sludged up *again*.

This time, I slapped myself in the head. In doing so, I propelled myself in a different direction.

I got rid of the tanks altogether and put in regular house plumbing. That third time removing the tanks wasn't long after the second time, so I thought, erroneously, it could not be that bad. I half-hearted the jetting process. As you may have guessed, the tank was full of sh…I mean, sludge. Lucky for me the maintenance people in the park where we stay were able to dispose of the black water tank for me, sludge and all.

The lesson here is — if you are in an RV, and have no plans to move it, get rid of the tanks. Someone recently moved into my park with a shiny, new fifth-wheel. The first thing they did was hire a guy to remove the tanks. If you do that, you also need to replace the RV toilet with a house toilet for an adequate flush. I should have done that the first time.

An RV toilet is designed to use the minimum amount of water so you don't fill the holding tank too quickly. The solid-to-water ratio makes it harder to dispose of the tank's contents when you dump. This lack of water promotes sludge buildup.

How RVs dump is by hooking the rig up to a sewer inlet access point provided by RV parks, and sometimes other locations such as truck stops. Theses inlets are designed to accept RV dump hose connectors. Portable RV sewer lines are made special for this. Dump hose kits and parts can be had anywhere RV stuff is sold.

Back to my nightmare. At the time, I thought since the tanks were accessible and I had the skills to repair them, I would be able to maintain them.

My mistake?

I did not account for the age of the tanks and the fact they were cheaply made. I also thought if we had to sell the rig, having the black water tank offered an advantage to the buyer.

I didn't consider the other practical realities. Our Carriage fifth-wheel is 26-years-old and 34-feet long. Cruising the country in such a rig isn't ideal. This rig *can* be moved, but it will never boondock or move far. Tanks for that rig don't make sense. Our home base rig is a sitter now.

Plenty of people want exactly that. Taking the tanks out actually *improves* its desirability in our local market. People who live in RVs don't want tank headaches. Our fifth-wheel rig is now a "5th Wheel a la Tiny House", optimized for full-time living. She wasn't designed to sit, but by happenstance, she does as do most of the rigs in this park. It was time to remove the tanks. We believe any rig that will sit long-term and be used only while stationary should have both waste tanks removed.

Keep in mind — smaller rigs and mobile rigs are easier to keep clean. Campers who motor about need tanks. Mobile motorhome gypsies have a good chance of maintaining their tanks appropriately. Rigs on the go need black water waste tanks, so the key is to care for them. If you can, try overnight boondocking without using the black tank for poop. There are always public toilets along the road while not in the wilds.

Waste Tank Tips

- Keep them clean! Clean them often, whether sitting or moving.
- Are your tanks getting iffy? Put a couple of bags of ice in the tank with some water and drive down a bumpy road. Ice will slosh and knock the crud off.
- Get a jetter wand (or make one) and keep it with your rig. Keep some hoses just for this purpose. Do not contaminate your potable hoses.
- When buying a rig, be aware of the black water tank location. In our 1990 Class-A, the tanks were on a platform in the basements alleviating strain on them. (And making them easily removable.) The three-inch waste pipe was located directly under the toilet and went straight down (no bends) so we saw the tank's true condition. RV toilets do not have a built-in trap, so when you flush it goes directly to the waste tank.
- Supported well and built with thick ABS, tanks should never need replacement but they seldom come that way.
- Think about tanks before you buy a rig. You must manage and deal with waste regularly as part of RV life.
- Understand the differences between the black and gray tank.
- The best and fastest way to learn how to dump tanks is to ask your fellow campers, the camp host, or the park maintenance guy.
- Here is my last bit of advice: Avoid pooping in the tank! That eliminates most of the tank problems. The less you poop in your tanks the better off you will be. Don't put toilet paper in there if you can avoid it. Use a trash can. And, if you must use paper, use single-ply paper only.
- When we travel, we use public restrooms wherever possible. Have I mentioned: Don't poop in the tank!

SECTiON TWO:

Road Strategies and Stories

Travel Logs and Loops

In our travels, we experienced a variety of 'loops.' Loops can end where they started or at a different location. Our loops launched from wherever we wintered, typically Florida but even Texas. Our biggest loop took a year. On that one our goal morphed into seeking the Four Corners. The Big Loop started and ended in what used to be our home territory of northeast Pennsylvania.

What exactly is a loop?

A loop is any trip launched from a home base situation. We'd split for an extended period of time and eventually return to home base for long-term parking. Our extended Four Corners loop took us 17,000 miles altogether starting in the Northeast, going through the south, back up north, back south again and on to winter in Texas where we decided on doing the Four Corners.

What are the Four Corners? It's where the four western states — Utah, Colorado, Arizona and New Mexico — collide in a geographic region. That was a dang big loop. We sure know how to act loopy.

Doing our loops, we usually had no definitive destination. We instead followed vague notions of where to go. We knew we wanted to go to the Four Corners but not when or where within it.

"Look at that," Lisa would often say while considering a distant point of interest such as an obscure national monument.

"It's on the way," I'd respond.

It took a long time to make that loop. There were too many interesting things to see and do between here and there, wherever here and there were.

Our Mutt-and-Jeff routine paid unbelievable dividends as we found things on the way you can't find with tourist brochures. The best stuff was the stuff we found in between the stuff we were trying to find. You will experience happy accidents on the road if you look for them as we did.

We started when GPS wasn't dependable, and oh boy, did we learn that the hard way!

I'm good with maps because I traveled a lot for work. I have always loved maps. We used an old Hagstrom Atlas to locate national and state points of interest. We'd look at the atlas with its obscure symbol markers that nobody looks at: historical markers, national monuments, and other oddball sites people have never heard of.

One of us would say the usual, "That looks interesting."

The other would say, "It's on the way."

We headed for them willy-nilly. We also employed a map program on the laptop to get us where we were going, but we were never concerned about arriving on time or if we ever made it there at all. Any side trip that looked good, we took. We eventually had the Corners in mind but we took a heck of a long zig-zag ride to get there.

| **TIP:** GPS is better today, but keep a map on board.

We've made a lot of circles. Lisa and I have a running joke. Every time we missed a turn (which used to happen often), we'd laugh about making yet another circle. It seems we can't go anywhere without first chasing our tails.

That's the point of looping. On the road, we didn't care about little circles. We created plenty of ringlet trips! We hereby designate these semi-aimless trips as loops.

Jump-Touring

Our next topic is jump-touring. This is big.

Want to know how to save money while having a good time doing it? This is our way.

When we left in our first RV, our available money decided how much we drove or parked. We based our budget on the rent of our former apartment. At the time, we paid $750. In today's market, that's cheap. That same apartment today is more like $2,000.

At the time, we thought to ourselves — if this lifestyle doesn't cost the same or less money, why bother? We needed to stick to our traditional budget first and foremost. It turned out that our regular budget was more than we needed. We saved money every month.

How?

Jump-touring.

We wanted to go everywhere. But we also exercised patience. We did not have a schedule. That is key. Where we went and where we stayed depended on the money. We'd sit at cheap places, like federal primitive campgrounds, for up to two weeks (the usual limit for federal camps) before moving on. If we didn't have a federal camp, we would do long-term boondocking to save money. We sought and found cheap out-of-the-way campgrounds in areas of less economic activity that offered better rates. Once we had reached our monetary goals, we moved on.

This technique made it possible to go to the higher-cost campgrounds when we had a reason to, like the ones we visited in Little Rock, Arkansas, and New Orleans, Louisiana.

We'd jump from place to place and stay wherever we landed as time and money allowed. We always used the best cost options.

There are several ways to get camp discounts. Here's what we did.

The Federal Access Pass offers savings, available for free to American citizens with disabilities. Seniors and veterans qualify, too. We had to learn where the cheap rates were on the fly because we didn't know the regions we visited. If you do nothing but bounce to and from federal sites, there is one for every price range from posh to primitive. Many primitive spots are free! And, the access pass sometimes provides free entry into federally controlled points of interest such as the Skyline Drive.

Since we first launched into our motorhome gypsy lifestyle, all kinds of phone apps and Internet sites have sprung out like mushrooms in cow poop to show you where the deals are. Apps are great. There are apps for everything: dump stations, truck stops, gas prices, Bureau of Land Management federal sites, federal parks, national monuments, Army Corps of Engineers campsites, state and local parks, camping stores, private parks, free overnight parking locations, and boondocking apps. We used all the above places.

It's hard to beat a camping club discount membership. A one-year membership in the discount camping club Passport America cost us $49 a year at the time. What's a camping club? It's an organization that lists locations of discount camping for club members in regular campgrounds. Camping clubs, like Passport America, Good Sams, Escapees, and others provide great discounts. There are many such organizations. Each one has its plus and minus columns.

> **TIP:** Our membership paid for itself in savings after two campground stays.

We used Passport America and will again. At the time, Passport gave us a big fat booklet with 3,000 commercial campgrounds listed. It has an app now, but I like books. To date, they still make the book but you pay for shipping. We lived by that book. Whenever we needed to land for the Internet, or a dump station, or just a rest from the road, the discount book was our guide. The book lists member campgrounds' conditions to stay, facilities' offerings, and discount time limits. There won't be any discounts available on holidays, during big local events, or peak business times such as weekends.

Often camp club discounts are limited to the middle of the week, nothing better than an almost empty campground. The discount could run anywhere from a single night to up to five days. Discounts can get you half off! We did all we could to avoid weekend stays at busy parks anyhow. We like peace and quiet, and sometimes weekend campers party hardy. So, the odd-days-out discount worked perfectly. We'd roll into one of these places on a Monday when it was slow for them. Some campgrounds may even be cheaper and offer extended discounts in the early or late season before most weekend campers are camping. Some of the listed member campgrounds in our discount book only allowed discounts at certain times of the year. Off-season, we occasionally received an extended discount because the place was empty. It doesn't hurt to ask. Corporate chains won't give you a break, but privately-owned campgrounds can if they want to. To be fair, we generally did not use commercial campgrounds because of cost. In popular locations, you may as well rent a house. The only cheap camping in New Jersey, for example, is in the national and state forests, but they aren't *that* cheap. None of the commercial campgrounds we looked at in New Jersey offered club membership discounts.

A private campground at a discounted rate allows one an opportunity to soak up some rest and relaxation, check the email, have a drink at the clubhouse and get a good shower that's not at a truck stop. Sometimes, like we did in New Orleans, you can try the hot tub or pool before driving on. Why not?

Jump-touring stretches the gas, too. Our pattern went like this:

We would drive a while on our way someplace. Then, we would sit a while, and drive another tankful, before we sat there a while. We'd boondock between targeted locations. Those targeted locations were often federal lands that allowed us to stay cheap or free. The only real cost was food and gas. If you drive 500 or even 1000 miles in a month, gas isn't that bad. I know what you're thinking…

"But gas costs so much!"

When we launched, gas was at an all-time high, yet still cheaper than rent.

Out of gas money? No money for camps?

Drive less, boondock more. For us, we were able to save up to $500 a month at times, compared to our former rent. How can you beat it?

We motorhome gypsies do like our discounts, don't we?

What is boondocking?

Boondocking refers to parking overnight, usually for free, without hook-ups so you need to rely on your on-board systems. One can also boondock in campsites, be it a paid or a free spot. Camping people consider the word boondocking to refer to a free overnight stay. Overnight boondocking can be sketchy in public, high-population areas and even unsafe. That said, boondocking can also be a fantastic experience if you're smart. You will be surprised at how many properties allow boondocking: shopping centers, big box stores like Walmart, lumber and feed store chains, camp store chains, Cracker Barrel restaurants, and others. The free-overnight-parking apps will show you many more locations.

My favorite overnight spot is truck stops. You heard me, I said truck stops.

Yes, you have truck noise all night, trucks moving, lot lizards roaming, and midnight dog walkers.

But on the positive side, it is pretty safe. Women traveling in an RV like a safe spot. It's safe because of all that activity. No worries about cops, either. Everything you may need is there and — *this is big* — some truck stops have dump stations. Better yet, most truck stops have good showers for a small fee! The best showers ever! When you are tired, hungry, and shot to hell, there is nothing better than a real shower.

The new fancy truck stops built recently are a wonderland! Some of them have the best food you ever ate while others have terrible chain food. Personally, I never pass up a BBQ stand in a truck stop parking lot. Chain truck stops are everywhere. I have my favorite — on the east coast it's Love's, because of the coffee.

If you need to do repairs, like Lisa and I did on our Class-C, a truck stop parking lot offers the space and the safety to do it. They may even have some basic supplies in their store.

Remember that all day repair we did in a truck stop's parking lot? We took the front of that truck apart and scattered it everywhere. No problem. Don't try that in a box store's parking lot. I'm sure the truck stop's workers were talking about us inside.

"Did you see them crazy old ladies pulling a radiator? What a trip."

The girl that rents the showers looked at us with pity and a wry smile. She let us go in together — two for the price of one. She probably didn't want management to notice. Maybe it was payment for the entertainment we provided that day. God bless her. We were on a tight budget and that shower was pure luxury.

Let me explain something about chain truck stop showers. They are not what you may think. They are big enough for five people. The water is hot and endless and they give you towels. You take as long as you want, no meters! And most times, the place is clean and tidy, all tile. Perfect. The perfect shower.

To be fair, not all truck stops are created equal. The chains such as Pilot, TA and Love's are pretty much the same. They all have fast food, stores, and showers. They are safe. Some privately-owned truck stops can be nasty. The food might suck, which is rare, but they are usually safe as well. On the other hand, the opposite is also true — some privately-owned stops have the best, non-chain food you can get.

Need a boondock? Don't turn your nose up at truck stops.

Boondocking Basics

- Yes, get the apps to find locations.
- Use your best, good-neighbor manners. While boondocking you are a guest, so act like one!
- Clean up after yourself.
- We often go into the store or location where we are docking and ask the store manager if it's cool. We like to let management know we are there. This is not necessary in truck stops.
- Look for a level place out of the way.
- Do not hinder parking lot traffic or the store's operation in any way.
- Do not put leveling jacks down onto raw pavement. Use blocks as to not cause any harm.
- Putting out slides can be an issue for some lots so don't do that. Look like you are overnight parking, not like you are taking up residence. Don't set up the lawn chairs and bar-b-que in Wally-World's parking lot.
- We also tend to buy from the stores of the lots where we boondock. It's a win-win.

Monday Strategies

One benefit of rolling into any camp on a Monday — commercial or federal — is that people leave stuff behind. Firewood is common. I don't know about you, but I love a good campfire. Federal law states that one may not bring wood into or transport it out of any forest controlled by the federal government. The same rule often applies to state and some private campgrounds. Dead fall is fair game. Some places will sell you safe wood to burn, even federal sites, but it is not cheap. As much as I enjoy sawing and splitting bug-encrusted logs, it's nice when somebody else does it for me.

Weekend campers bring wood with them, despite the rules, and they'll leave the leftovers behind. Most sites will have a piece or two. Sometimes, the previous inhabitants leave a stack. We had bicycles with baskets for a reason. We'd pull in, setup, and take a little tour on the bikes. Yup, there is always wood to find.

The rules state that if firewood came from outside, it needs to be destroyed. Say...in a campfire, for example. Free wood is good wood. So, we help the park clean up after the weekenders a little, nothing wrong with that.

Of course, people leave all sorts of things behind. Whenever we came upon anything of value, we've always turned it in at the camp office. Motorhome gypsies are not thieves, despite what Cher's famous song "Gypsies, Tramps and Thieves" might make you think. (I'm dating myself here, oops!)

One time, on a motorcycle tour along the Colorado River in Utah, near Moab, we pulled into a free park on federal land. We had just come from climbing cliffs to see dinosaur footprints. There were restrooms and kiddy park stuff in the pull-over area, lovely as can be. Sitting on a wall facing the river, I spotted a change purse on a rock. It was a nice leather bag, well made.

I retrieved it and found foreign coins inside. I could not find an office or visitor's center or anywhere with an attendant or a lost-and-found to return it. The federal office could be anywhere in the Moab, Utah region. We started asking around, but failed to find the owner. Eventually we found a ranger at Arches, he said to keep it. We still have it, and the coins.

Keep your eyes open everywhere. I've found money and valuables in parking lots many times, especially in gravel parking lots at gemstone and fossil joints. I found some nice crystals somebody dropped one time. You can't take fossils or petrified wood off any federal land, but you can buy samples all over the place. I bought myself a couple of trilobites at one stop.

Life as a motorhome gypsy allows you to go and enjoy without spending a lot of money doing it. Spending less has anyone's best interests in mind. We made a game of stretching out the budget and getting the most out of every experience and every dime. Campsite people do share. People have given me things I needed, and I have done the same. Campers share items, but they also share great tips on where to go next.

Perhaps you won't get many ideas from other campers on an empty Monday, but the camp host or site employees will have time to tell what they know. While picking up firewood why not pick a brain or two as well?

Visiting New Orleans

After we arrived in Florida, for the second or third time, we camped around Florida, hitting both coasts before and after time with Lisa's parents. We made many return trips to Florida and even went down to Key West on one. This travel log email below is how things fell out upon leaving Florida in the off-season.

We decided to hit New Orleans on our way west after leaving Florida.

We stayed at an RV park on Lake Pontchartrain near New Orleans. The park was outside of the city with industrial docks and shipping around us. The park's site spacing was tight, but since off-season had started, it wasn't full. This campground has a bar on site with food. They even have a free shuttle bus that goes into the French Quarter three times a day!

Lisa and I aren't the drinking type, but there was plenty to do and see in New Orleans without drinking. We are musicians and love music, so this was a great stop for us. We got to see what the town is like without the distraction of revelers.

We did have a couple of overpriced meals there in New Orleans, but we also found better food cheaper. This stop introduced us to the shrimp po-boy sandwich, which we enjoyed greatly and is now on our list of favorites.

We spent three days in New Orleans, and we felt that was all we needed to see and enjoy the place. When the discount ran out, we ran out, too.

When in a new, touristy place, we ask the locals where they eat. That's how you get a few bucks off the tourist prices and a taste of the real local flavors.

New Orleans

From Rachel's Email:

It's weird—we get to New Orleans and it's 38 degrees, a nice temperature for Boston this time of year. The sky is clear with no smog—also weird. What's really weird is the French Quarter. The place was almost empty last night. The only revelers were a few old hippies and a woman with a tick. Yet the place was alive with bands, all playing to empty bars.

This allowed me to really see the place, as there were not many people to distract us. The architecture is interesting but less special without all the craziness hanging off balconies. That's the kind of thing for which this place is famous. Normally, tourists go crazy while in town. We didn't see any of that.

It occurs to me that this place is just another place.

Who knew you could have a quiet introspective time sitting in a New Orleans bar? (This is why we love traveling off-season.)

As I write this, it's 10 a.m. We are about to take the shuttle bus into town for the last time. We'll see more of the place in broad daylight. I'll watch the lone street performers play to the spirits of Bourbon Street. No one else will be looking except the eagle-eyed cops and us. Because it's so cold, we'll hit the museums and art galleries.

I learned something about New Orleans. If you want that good ol' southern food, don't get it here, because it costs three times more than the ma and pa shops outside the city. I'll wait until I'm 50 miles down the road to get oysters and mudbugs. I'll pass on the 10-dollar cup of beer.

My enjoyment here is what I see, anyway, mostly architecture. There is just enough weirdness added to make New Orleans more than just another place. And who knows, I may get to see some weirder people today. (Or maybe regular people acting weird.) Tomorrow, we head west.

~ Rachel

After New Orleans and Holly Springs[5]

From Rachel's Email:

After New Orleans, we wandered a bit west and then turned north. The truck was still running hot. We were yet to resolve our overheating problems. The cold temps kept us in the running, but driving with a hot motor wasn't relaxing. So, we headed toward colder weather—not a typical strategy for motorhome gypsies.

In northern Mississippi, we stayed at a federal forest, Holly Springs, with Indian mounds and a big, beautiful lake. People hear the word "Mississippi" and think of flat swampland. We discovered the north to be a series of hills and conifer trees. The campground was surrounded by natural landscape which made it feel primitive in a good way. We had full hook-ups despite rustic appearances, just how we like it. The place was nearly empty. We stayed two weeks.

This campground was dead midweek and came alive on weekends when the locals swarmed the lake.

I can't forget this park specifically because of one man, the fake camp host. Camp hosts are volunteers that help manage a campground. In exchange for their services, usually not very difficult work (cleaning bathrooms, showing people to their sites), they get a free campsite and other perks. What they receive varies depending on how much work they are required to do. Some hosts get liquified petroleum gas for free and a little stipend. Camp hosts usually stay one season, but some stay for years.

We met a couple at a campfire one night. He was an older man, older than 60 is my guess, and she was a 30-something hippie chick, long hair, long skirt, puffy blouse and love beads.

---

5 This email was sent before we decided on the Four Corners. Unknown to us at the time, we were already on the Big Loop. We had crossed the Mississippi seven times and covered thousands of miles before limping back to Pennsylvania.

This guy was a trip, full of stories. He
produced a beat-up Gibson guitar and then
proceeded to tell us it had belonged to B.B.
King when B.B.'s house burned down. He made some
crazy claims about his association with B.B.
and his life in general—said he was a surgeon
in Vietnam, a roadie for the Grateful Dead, and
other wild tales. The entire time, he was drunk.

The next day, he was sitting on a golf cart
holding a one-gallon milk jug, full of beer
with a big head on it. He claimed it was "apple
juice with foam". (In most federal campgrounds,
alcohol is not allowed. In some parks, you
can, but not this one.) Meanwhile, the place
was buzzing with rangers doing seasonal jobs.
They weren't there for campground operations.
The work involved property maintenance.

It didn't take long before we discovered
"Mr. Fuzzy Apple Juice" was a fake camp host
living in the real camp host's storage shed.
The real camp host had his fifth-wheel locked
and parked next to the shed. Where the real
host went, I'll never know, but Mr. Fuzzy Apple
Juice Guy was an entertaining replacement.

When we left Mississippi, we continued
our zig-zagging. The truck's overheating got
worse. We decided to head east to deal with
the mechanicals. On the way, of course, we
found some more interesting things, like the
campground with a rifle range we stopped at in
Tennessee. We were able to borrow a gun and
shoot the hell out of those tin cans.

The best zig-zag for me was in Ohio. We were
100 miles from a bicycle museum when we learned
of it while on the road. It was a private
collection of antique bicycles. Even though it
was technically out of our way, we went anyway.
It blew my mind—I used to collect antique
pedal bicycles and motorcycles. I love them.

This place had the best collection I've ever
seen. The docent noticed me bubbling over with
excitement and took me downstairs to show me
the overflow. You know, the bikes that are not

CAMPGROUND GOTHIC

on display. Hundreds of them! Rare bikes, unique bikes, bikes you never heard of, even bikes from the 1890s boom of bicycle innovations.

Lisa is not a bike freak, but even she could not help but be impressed.

See you in Pa.,

~ Rachel

The Big Loop

We had many loops during our first three years on the road. Some were local to the east coast and the south. We didn't get much into the upper middle of the country. The Shenandoah Valley and the Blue Ridge Parkway were favorite stays of ours, although on occasion we stayed in commercial campgrounds in that region. Our Big Loop began in Pa. but stalled. After fixing the truck, we went south for the winter before going north and west in the early spring. After restarting we ended up in Aransas Pass, Texas, where we stayed for two months.

Wintering in Aransas Pass on the Gulf coast in Texas is where we decided on the Corners. The Four Corners region is chock full of federal reserves and parks. Many of the big, well-known places are there.

I don't have much to say about Aransas, other than it was dirt cheap and the seafood was to die for. We often went to a fish shack on the docks to have the day's catch right out of the Gulf of Mexico. They sold a giant plate of oysters so cheap we'd eat a dozen each. I've never had better fish or shellfish, and I grew up on the bay at the Jersey shore.

When it was time, still early in the season, we started north for the Corners from there.

Leaving Texas took a long time because Texas is a big-ass state. We camped three times before reaching New Mexico. Each Texas stop was prolonged and interesting. Stockton, Texas, for example, was a dust bowl and practically deserted, but it had its charms. In the 1890s, Stockton was a big deal town so we found interesting Victorian architecture. There was money to be had in cattle and oil back then, which made some folks rich, and as a result, they brought the town up. In its day, it had a train station, nice hotel, government offices, and fine houses. I found another big surprise — a free museum with everything from fossils to geological stuff, from Western United States history to Native American history, and the history of the oil industry.

I also got a fancy haircut there by the only gay man within 100 miles, at least as far as we could tell. This hair stylist grew up in that town and offered a strange juxtaposition after having tracked across red-neck country full of conservatives.

Another memorable Texas stop on our way out of Aransas Pass was at a brand-new Army Corps of Engineers site near Grainger, Texas, on a lake near another almost dead cowboy town. Here, too, the buildings were fascinating. The place seemed like a movie set. I later learned it *was* used in the movies.

One cool camp stop was on the Pecos River near Barstow, Texas. The thing I recall most was that crispy, new shower house — because it didn't have hot water! The campground was empty except for one old-timer living in his van and a man at the entry gate.

From there, we headed to Carlsberg Caverns, New Mexico. That was a long drive! The most exciting thing we saw were jackrabbits playing dodgeball with tumbleweeds. We enjoyed Carlsberg's gigantic cave systems, but it wasn't a long stay. How many times can one tour a big-ass cave? We weren't really in the Corners yet, but this site is considered by some to be a part of the experience.

Being an author of science fiction, I was interested in UFO lore. Of course, we had to go to Roswell, New Mexico. Incidentally, at the Roswell UFO library, you might find one of my political cartoons that had been published in a now-defunct Lehigh Valley newspaper, *Bethlehem News.*[6] The illustration features aliens in the lawn care business. I sent them the framed original. I liked Roswell, but there wasn't much to see other than the UFO stuff.

During our boondocking stay at a Walmart parking lot in Roswell, I noticed the lot was half full of people living there. Many were van dwellers with no other residence. It was sad to see so many people so poor. We saw a lot of that in our travels.

In the same parking lot, there were some big rigs, meaning, rigs owned by people with money. Our rig was old and looked like it. The way we see it is this: Who gets robbed first, the beat-up 1978 truck people or the $100,000 Class-A people?

When beggars came to our door asking for money, I laughed.

"Are you kidding?" I said, "I'm broke, but I can give you some food."

They didn't want the food.

One of our safety strategies is to blend in and it worked. We were doing fine, but we never wore that on our sleeves. We do usually give money or food to those in need, but not always. You have to be cautious in a parking lot full of desperation.

---

6   *Publisher's note:* Rachel Thompson and I met when I was the managing editor of The Lehigh Valley News Group. I hired her and trained her as a freelance reporter.

Roswell, the Valley of Fire, and the Three Rivers Petroglyph

From Rachel's Email: Written March 19

After leaving Roswell, we went west on Route
380, an amazing ride due to the landscape.
Along 380, we wandered between juniper-covered
hills and steadily climbed to more than 6,000
feet. The landscape changed from low desert
to high plains. Mesas popped up, and distant
snow-covered mountains were all around.

Finally, we saw a bit of the 19th century
Wild West: working ranches, old adobe ruins
along the road, and wide-open spaces. As we
traveled, hills took over the flats. We passed
through several historic towns set between
rises such as Pikachu, Hondo, and Capitan. We
stopped at a few vistas, saw some big active
ranches, (and lots of coyotes) as we drove
through Lincoln County.

The town of Lincoln was cool. It had a
stretch of old west cowboy-time buildings
along with museums and other attractions. Billy
the Kid called it home for a time. The hill
country around it was intense. After Lincoln
and Capitan, we descended from the taller
hills onto a rolling high plain.

The Valley of Fire, our next destination,
is a federal campground five miles west of
Carrizozo, a way down from the hill passes.
Carrizozo, in its heyday, was a booming
railroad town that employed 150 men. Now,
about five people work for the railroad. This
according to the 90-year-old camp host who
lived there during the boom-to-bust cycle.
Carrizozo was not much like other big towns we
saw. (Big is a relative term. This place had
a dozen buildings at best.) Thankfully, there
were a lot fewer corporate representations,
very few neon signs and plenty of locally-
owned businesses, and the best part, no
Walmart! The diner, or café as they called it,

served great home-cooked food, free wi-fi, and really nice people.

What is the Valley of Fire?

It is 44-miles long and spans from 2 to 20 miles wide. It's a 5,000-year-old, dead lava flow, making it the most recent lava field in the continental United States.

The campground itself is situated on an island of sandstone that the lava flowed around. We sat high above a sea of twisted black rocks and similarly twisted dwarf trees and plants. We camped at Valley of Fire for a few nights. Valley of Fire is a Bureau of Land Management site that floored us. (We would have liked to stay longer, and so much so that we later returned to it). It was a great camping site. Excellent showers, level parking, and a three-quarter mile path in the lava fields for a closer look.

The animal and plant life there was just wild. There were educational displays along the walking path elaborating on the fauna and explaining how the Native Americans used the flora. It was a testimony to the ingenuity of the Native Americans. They even made alcoholic drinks from a certain desert plant.

Who knew?

It is hard to believe people not only survived but thrived in this environment. We saw black rock Squirrels, hawks, and a lot of tracks from mule deer, cougar, coyote, kit fox, and ringtail cats. We also saw some tarantula spider burrows. Thankfully for Lisa, it was too cold for spiders. Lisa hates bugs, so that makes me the official bug-killer—but not on federal lands where the rule is to do no harm, take nothing, and leave nothing. This hands-off policy preserves pristine natural environments.

From Valley of Fire, we headed south 30 miles on Route 54 to the Three Rivers Petroglyph site. This is a national monument location with just two free campsites, and we got one. Yeah us! I learned about Three Rivers in the stack of archeology magazines I bought from a thrift shop in Texas. The article explained there were more than 21,000 native rock art examples and that almost anyone could find one not yet recorded.

It was out of our way, but we just had to go. That's the kind of nerds we are.

The petroglyphs were situated on a mile-and-a-half long trail along the top ridge of a collapsed mesa. These volcano-blasted, black rock hills were smothered in petroglyphs. (The rocks had a black patina. Indigenous Americans would scratch that black coating away to draw a picture.) We saw and touched them, up close and personal. The first day, we only went up for a few hours as we got in late. The next day, we spent a whole eight-hour day in the hills. I made sketches, and Lisa took pictures. We climbed among 4,000 years' worth of Native American tribal art. We learned later that almost every place where petroglyphs exist is strictly hands-off. You can't even get close. But here you are invited to see them up close.

Mind you, we were a long way from the nearest town. Right out on Route 54 where it turns off into the national park, there was a gift shop. Actually, it was way more than a gift shop. It's an art museum with first-rate art of all kinds mixed with Western antiques of excellent quality. I saw a rare antique pistol that I'm sure is worth $5,000.

After that side trip, we stayed at Valley of Fire again to stock up on water, dump the tanks, and get a hot shower.

After leaving Valley of Fire for the second time, I renamed Interstate 25. I call it the Beer Bottle Highway. I never saw so many beer bottles along the road in my life. I was scared to drive there. I later understood the bottles were deposited over a long time as there is no money or local interest in keeping the highways

clean.[7] Nothing changes much in the desert
over time as the many ruins, weathered wood,
steel of antique cars, and adobe buildings
demonstrate.

Bottle collectors, get you out west!
—Rachel

---

7   I later learned the reservation nearby did not allow alcohol so the Native Americans
would leave the property to have a drink, or two, or three, off the reservation.

Albuquerque to Grants, to El Malpais, New Mexico

from email:

Grants, New Mexico, is another poor, disheveled place mostly inhabited by Native Americans. We ate at the worst Denny's Restaurant ever. Their eggs were crispy, the toast burnt, and the bacon chewy as shoe leather. That toast would make nice roof tiles. Everywhere we went, the places near Native American towns and reservations had higher prices and terrible quality even in chain restaurants.

We went to Albuquerque for one main reason. We had gotten hooked on petroglyphs, and we had to see more. The Indian Petroglyph National Monument is located in Albuquerque. So, we found a Walmart near the site and camped overnight. This allowed us to get the truck's oil changed, shop for food, and get to the bank for a few rolls of laundry quarters. We had to pass this way anyway, so it looked like a good stop.

It wasn't.

The Indian Petroglyph National Monument was a total disappointment. The rock arts were few and far between, and we had to stay on a sandy path at the bottom of the rock formations. The path was covered in broken glass and old shotgun shells. We would have to have hiked a lot more miles to see a small number of petroglyphs compared to what we saw at Three Rivers. After hiking a mile, we called it off.

But the hike was not without merits. We did see a lot of tracks and dung, and we made a game of identifying the animals that had left their marks. We figured out various types of lizard tracks after seeing one lizard shoot off under a shrub. We saw spider footprints and other bug prints, too. This fine sand was good for tracking tiny creatures.

Who knew?

Oddly, the highlight was leaving the park and going on to a commercial campground ten miles outside of Albuquerque right off Interstate 40 going west. It's always nice to land someplace interesting rather than sleeping in Walmart parking lots. This place, Enchanted Trails, had a great laundry with a game room attached, good showers, and a free pool table.

The gift shop was well stocked, and I found a little beaded pouch for cheap with a Route 66 motif on it. (I still have and use that change purse today!) The old Route 66, of the Bob Dylan song fame, runs along I-40 here. The best part, the camp office had a huge collection of antique toys and 1950s furniture with all kinds of household items from the 50s. The collection continued backward to the late Victorian age.

Yeah, you guessed it, another free museum. The owner specialized in camp-related collectibles. I saw a number of very, very rare, camp-related toys. They also had some restored antique cars hooked to campers from the 1930s and 40s. It's not every day you see a

Hey, get a pic of this butterfly.

'47 Hudson replete with a matching '47 teardrop travel trailer.

And to add convenience to pleasure, the campground stood right next door to the chain store Camper's World, where we stocked up on some RV stuff that we needed.

Next, we drove on to Grants, the so-called big town in the middle of no place along I-40. Can't say much about Grants because there is nothing much there, but the ride to it was fantastic, a landscape to die for. Grants is located just above where we wanted to go next. We boondocked there and left early the next morning.

And where might we have been heading, you ask?

Why . . . El Malpais National Monument, of course.

Our method of how to decide where to go was established long before we turned off the big road, Interstate 40 in New Mexico, onto a county road, Route 53 in Grants. Upon leaving Albuquerque and heading west, we looked at the map, pointed at a couple of relatively unknown national monuments, picked one randomly, and said the usual thing to each other.

"That looks good. Let's go."

"It's on the way."

As George Harrison said in a song "When you don't know where you're going, any road will take you there".

Hey, it worked before.

We wanted to get off the big super slab and row our boat in a slower creek. You get tired of open road highways. The old truck didn't go that fast and speeds are crazy. We figured why use the interstate if we aren't in a hurry?

We took any opportunity to get off the beaten path. The off-the-beaten-path road we took this time pointed indirectly at the national monument, El Morro, our next planned destination.

Route 53 was the long scenic route heading towards El Morro by way of El Malpais. Route 53 first took us into and through El Malpais

National Monument and its wild volcanic
landscape. Early spring, and we didn't realize
that this road went straight into a dead
volcanic mountain range. What a pleasant
surprise. Fantastic tall pine scenery!

There was snow up in them thar hills, and
worse at the top. It had snowed recently. It
threatened to do it again. The roads were
already sketchy. No other car was anywhere to
be seen for long miles.

El Malpais was not exactly a stop. It was
supposed to be a drive-through situation but
we stopped anyway. The park starts as a low
volcanic field, which we drove out of and into
a mountain range. We hit about 8,000 feet
at the top where there was a lot of snow
on the ground. It was a very pretty, old-
growth ponderosa pine forest with interesting
foliage that we had not seen before in lower
elevations. We stopped at the ranger station
and talked with a very enthusiastic park ranger
who worked the tourist gift shop/visitor center/
ranger station. That sweetheart volunteer gave
us a lot of good local information. She and
other volunteers do embroidery on baseball
caps of good quality that the feds provide.
They sell them at various visitor centers which
benefit the parks. I bought one with a cougar on
it and I still have it.

Meow.

The best part? She told us about nearby campgrounds and the nearest is called the Ice Cave.

Ice Cave was a great stop for artifact nerds
like me. That site turned out to be fantastic.
We would not have known about it if not for the
park volunteer.

Bless her heart.

The Ice Cave campground blew us away. It
was vacant being so early in the spring, but
everything was open. They had a lot to offer
including the best Native American artifacts
I ever saw.

The Ice Cave and Bandera Volcano are located in the west-central Zuni Mountain range of New Mexico, where N.M. State Hwy 53 crosses the North American Continental Divide. Our GPS coordinates are 35° 00.002'N by 108° 04.388'W at the entrance to our driveway off Hwy 53, and 34° 59.592'N by 108° 04.836'W at our front door. The location on a highway map is N.M. State Hwy 53, 25-26 miles southwest of Grants, N.M. from Exit 81 on I-40. Our mailing address is 12000 Ice Caves Rd. Grants, N.M. 87020. Historically, we are located along the Zuni-Acoma Trade Route and Coronado's Trail, likely Chacoan outlier site. If you see these signs, you are here. — *source: icecaves.com*

This privately owned place had been owned by the same family since the late 1890s. The Ice Cave itself, and park's namesake, is a volcanic tube of solid ice 40-feet deep that never melts. It's about 30 feet straight down from the surface. To get down to the ice, they provided a set of ladders and scaffolding. They have an awesome museum full of rare artifacts. How did they get this stuff? It was a major stopping place for Indians who used the cave to preserve food and they also hid non-food supplies all over there. The Spanish conquistadors had made camps on the property while searching for gold. One famous Spaniard left behind a rare ceramic wine jug which he had brought with him from Spain. Spanish armor and later cowboy artifacts were also found on the property and preserved by the owners. They have a fantastic collection of Anasazi pottery and artifacts including staves for making bows, arrow shafts, arrow heads and other materials found on the grounds over 100 years ago.

I've seen a lot of rare pottery but this collection takes the cake. The condition and unusual nature of the items from the site are extraordinary. I don't think they know the true value of what they have. I saw this painted ladle in perfect condition. I've seen a broken smaller example in a museum. I'm guessing they had half a million dollars, and likely more, in rare Anasazi pottery.

Bandera Volcano is on the property, too. A steep, half-mile hike got us up to the volcano's caldera with fantastic views along the winding trail. We saw the oldest known Douglas Fir tree in America along the way, said to be more than 700-years-old.

From the top of the caldera, we saw eleven of the region's thirteen volcanoes. Not bad for nine bucks a head.

The snow finally melted after a couple of days, and even though I could not get enough of this place, it seemed like a good time to go. We didn't want to get snowed in, again.

Benito and Regina Baca *(from their website)*

The Ice Cave family can trace our history to Manuel Antonio Candelaria (1837 – 1888) who was captured by the Navajos near Cubero, N.M. at the age of 9. He was later gambled to the Apache and lived with them until he left at the age of 19. He then returned to Cubero and his Spanish heritage. Manuel Antonio Candelaria married Regina Baca, daughter of Benito Baca who homesteaded Agua Fria near the Ice Caves. Here Benito Baca ran a small trading post. Due to raids by the Navajo and hard winters, Manuel moved his family to Concho, Arizona. After a time, Benito Baca moved to Concho and abandoned the homestead at Agua Fria. The land that includes Agua Fria and the Ice Caves was eventually purchased by Sylvestre Mirabal in 1915.

Regina Baca Candelaria and Manuel Antonio Candelaria

In the Concho Valley, Manuel was considered one of the Apache and was allowed to live peacefully there. It was there that he began a successful sheep business with his sons. During this time, he had a large family, ran a general store, opened one of the first banks in Northern Arizona, and secured over 100,000 acres of land for his sheep. When Manuel passed, his oldest son Juan took over the family business. Juan along with Sylvestre Mirabal envisioned joining their vast land holdings by arranging the marriage of Juan's three oldest sons to Sylvestre's three oldest daughters. *source: icecaves.com*

The folks at the Ice Cave directed us off the
mountain. We drove out of the high country
and into a desert prairie setting, mesas in
the distance. We continued towards El Morro,
a federal monument site that also offered
camping.

On the way we stopped at Ancient Way Café
to get a bite and stayed a week in their
campground We hated to leave when we did. One
of the best stops we ever had. I'll tell you
all about Ancient Way and El Morro in another
email.

~ Rachel

Ancient Way Café & Campground[8] and El Morro

from email:

It's March 22, and Lisa and I just got back from
hiking. We are in the Natural Bridges National
Park. I'm so tired but I wanted to get this
down. The cold air and 7500-foot elevation kicked
my ass. But I figure I better do this one before
I see too many more wonders, else, I forget.

When we were up on top of El Malpais, we
had stopped in at the ranger station to take a
break. The woman there told us about another
private campground below the mountains. No
details, just that it was a good place and
only a mile from our destination, El Morro.
We debated about going to a paid campground
when a free one was near and we were stocked
for boondocking. It was cold so we figured on
hitting the paid site for a night and using
our portable electric heater. Free heat is a
good thing.

There was a small complex of buildings
around the campground entrance. The camp
office/dinner turned out to be a popular eatery
and local meeting place we later learned. A
poetry group was meeting there when we went
inside.

The café is 100 yards away from the local
cultural center across the street—also used
as an art gallery called the Old School House.
It was just that, a one-room schoolhouse.
Next to that was a little business, a guy who
builds and sells sheds. We met him later and
hit it off well, a very nice fellow, indeed. He
gave us a lot of information about the region
and off-grid living. He told us all about the
local hippie commune and local Native American
reservation and said that we would fit in well.

And, we did.

---

8   The Ancient Way Café & Campground story appears elsewhere but we like the flavor
of this account and it has things not mentioned before.

We quickly learned Ancient Way is a bastion of love and acceptance. People from miles around come to the café because the food is amazing, healthy and cheap. The first time we entered the café, a very brutish-looking man sat near. He turned out to be a nice guy who worked 50 miles away. It felt odd at the time because this guy was an armed forest ranger in a café run by a very flamboyantly gay couple. From that first meal, I knew the place was a melting pot. The customers who came in and out were rough outdoorsmen, park service workers, local ranchers, local hippies and Native Americans from a nearby reservation.

Back to this rustic camp office building…I knew something was cool about this campground even before going inside. They had rainbow flags flying out front and locals on the front porch using computers—the kind of folks that reminded me of liberals from the Northeast. You know, an older guy with a ponytail that you just know drives a 1983 Volvo. Inside was old hippie heaven coated in queer frosting.

Cool art on the walls, a great mix of people, aromas of food to die for, lots of great big smiles, and treatment like we were lost family. It immediately felt like home. The atmosphere was full of goodwill. The spirit of love and acceptance spiced the mountain air. Within ten minutes, we were an ingrained part of the scenery.

The camp manager, Monki, was quick to point out that although the place is gay-owned, it's not a gay campground. Rather, it's an everyone-is-welcome place. Really, really welcomed. I asked Monki (pronounced Mahn-key, not Mun-key) how it was that in the middle of the great Southwest redneck wasteland everyone got along.

"Life is too hard up in the mountains to care what or who people are," he replied.

This place proved it well. I loved how Jerry Garcia and Janis Joplin posters blended with original local art pieces on the walls which were for sale. Hippie-era songs from 1964 into the mid-1970s played in the background. Led Zeppelin, the Beatles, the Rolling Stones and Fleetwood Mac ushered in the digestion of a good meal.

Monki ran the place. Standing Feather, possibly a gender-queer person, served tables in makeup and earrings glowing with friendly enthusiasm. The Native American cook came out of the kitchen to greet people. A transsexual Native American woman ran the cash register. I took to Standing Feather and Monki like they were my own long-missed family.

The clientele were locals of all flavors: gay, straight, Native American, Mexican, and redneck-white, all mixed together like happy jelly beans. I even met a white lawyer who works for the Navajo Nation—not your typical attorney. Monki introduced us to Susan, a disabled vet building a retreat for other disabled vets. After a two-hour coffee chat with Susan and others, we made camp.

The next day, we bicycled to El Morro.

El Morro does have camping, but no hook-ups. We were fine staying at Ancient Way so our worry about getting a spot there was moot. Camping in the federal-owned park would have been cheaper, but sometimes it's better to pay. Ancient Way was very reasonable.

El Morro National Monument was a little dot we found on the map. At the time, it looked like a good place to stop for a night of free camping. You've heard about the big National Parks like Yellowstone or Arches, but not so much about the little spots like this. This

The Headland Trail is 2 miles long and takes approximately 2 hours. You must start the trail no later than 3 pm. — *https://www.nps.gov/elmo/index.htm*

The Inscription Rock Trail is 0.75 miles (1.2km) long and takes approximately 45 minutes. You must start the trail no later than 4 pm

is a relatively small park, but the history is huge. El Morro is a mesa that once hosted a Native American Zuni Pueblo where more than 800 inhabitants lived on top of this mesa. We took the hike up to see it.

The steep-trail hike up to the ruins was too pretty to describe. I loved the rock formations with their array of colors and textures set against an endless blue sky and contrasted by soft green foliage. Made from local materials, the ruins blended perfectly with the environment. Too bad only the foundations remained. These Native American ruins are something every anthropology/ archeology geek should see. Everyone else would probably benefit from a visit, too. That long, steep climb to the top is good exercise!

If you walk the Inscription Rock Trail, you will see why El Morro was proclaimed a national monument. This trail takes you to a freshwater pool where hundreds of Spanish and early American inscriptions, as well as pre—historical petroglyphs, were carved into the mesa's rock face at ground level. If you still have time when you return to the visitor center, watch the 15-minute videos in the museum about each feature.

Native Americans chose this spot for good reason. Not only was it high and offered a good view of where the enemy might be, but the land below was rich with resources. At the base of the mesa stands a deep, rock-basin pool that collects rainwater and snow melt. It never goes dry because of how the surrounding geology protects it. The mesa's rock-basin pool provided the most important water supply for Native American tribes in the greater region.

It also saved the Spanish conquistadors from dying of thirst on their trek inland seeking gold, which was new information for me. We learned that the Spanish were all over this part of New Mexico. They left a trail of artifacts in the area, including discarded armor and swords.

Tourists can see some of these artifacts and learn the deep history at the El Morro Visitor Center located below the mesa.

The base of El Morro had long been a Native petroglyph repository. When others came, they too left their marks. Various well-known Spaniards wrote their hopes and dreams in an elaborate script carved in sandstone. Settlers, the American pony soldiers, and 20th-century passersby made their mark as well. Some are simple inscriptions scrawled with a piece of bone while others were carved masterfully and bore detailed messages. An early nineteenth-century New Mexico governor even had a plaque carved into El Morro by professional stone sculptors.[9] All carving into Inscription Rock, as it is known, was stopped by federal order in 1906.

After a long day on El Morro, it was back to Ancient Way and a hot shower.

The best part of seeking El Morro was our surprise and delight in finding Ancient Way. The second-best part was the open mic they held across the street in an old, one-room wooden school house a short walk away.

That night the Old School House Gallery's open microphone night was a hoot. Five bucks to get in, unless you performed. Then, they let you in free. We paid anyway. They had food and drink for a low price as well.

---

9   The Spanish governor of New Mexico was first to carve his name in 1605. His name is Don Juan de Qnate who wrote: "Here was the Señor and Governor Don Manuel de Silva Nieto, whose indubitable arm and valor have now overcome the impossible with the wagons of the King Our Lord, a thing which he alone put into effect, August 5, 1629, that one may well to Zuni pass and carry the faith."

The place was small but packed. Everyone living nearby came, about 50 people. Almost everyone did something to add to the show. The night was a mix of a lot of cool stuff. I read from my new novel and it was well-received. Lisa played guitar and sang a song. One woman wore a long gown and did an interpretive dance. Next, someone sang Elvis very well, while a small group of ten-year-old kids danced to the tune. A different set of kids sang next, followed by a poet who read a selection of his work and it was really good. A guy played guitar and sang. A group did a scarf dance that was a total riot. Another group performed a scene from a play. Monki in drag was one of the actors. All of them did a damn good job of acting and singing. I clapped so hard my hands hurt.

In the final act, a guy talked about the Reverend Fred Phelps and his Westboro Baptist Church (Of the "God Hates Fags" fame). He then commented on the Supreme Court's recent ruling on a suit, which Phelps won. The guy ended his eloquent talk by reading the lyrics from a gay composer's song entitled, "Fuck You." I wish I could remember the composer's name.

At the end of the night, we all went outside to watch a Native fire dancer do his art. Amazing! I've never seen a native fire-dancer do his thing in person. It touched me deeply. I'll never forget the flames whirling, and his face glowing by the firelight. The stars sprinkled illumination across the moonless night for our walk home. It was a perfect evening.

When we broke camp, I didn't want to go. I wanted to stay forever. But there was a reprieve on the road outbound. We had been invited to Susan's place, and we decided to take her up on the offer. Even the 20-mile drive to her house proved worth the trip, we passed

Native American ruins and beautiful landscapes. Susan's home also had a wonderful view.

The breakfast she prepared for us extended into a delightful four-hour brunch. We talked as Susan cooked. It was a great conversation upstaged by Susan's excellent food.

The entire region of northwest New Mexico, from the people to the high places, had conspired to enchant Lisa and I.

Weeks later as I write this from Natural Bridges, we talk of going back. We try finding a reason to visit again. It wasn't on the way to anywhere we were heading, so we didn't make it back. Perhaps, someday, we'll return. Standing Feather said he went to Ancient Way for a week and stayed four years, so far, with no plans of leaving. I see how that can happen. I can see it happening to us.

What About Natural Bridges?

We wrote about El Morro and our adventures there from Natural Bridges several weeks after leaving. Natural Bridges is another federal site which will forever remain fixed in my mind. You'll see why from our email below. As we progressed on our way to the Four Corners, we first had many more stops before arriving there. Natural Bridges was one of the standouts. The Painted Desert/Petrified Forest was our next big federal park stop after El Morro.

Painted Desert/Petrified Forest:

While wintering in Texas, we had decided to see Moab, Utah but first we had much to see on our way. From El Morro in Ramah, New Mexico, we headed west for the Painted Desert in Arizona. We were later diverted from reaching Moab after leaving the Painted Desert due to mechanical problems and side trips. Off the beaten track again, we took advantage of that unexpected detour and visited Colorado but I'm getting ahead of myself.

In northern Arizona, one can explore a series of national monuments often grouped with the Grand Canyon, on the west side of the state: The Painted Desert, the Petrified Forest, and Canyon De Chelly, were within or near the Navajo Nation on the east side of New Mexico close to the border. To reach the Painted Desert with its remnants of fossilized trees, travelers cross the Petrified Forest National Park. From the visitor's center's outlooks, amazing views from there, you can see parts of historic Route 66. The area is full of Triassic fossils.

We began our visit via Interstate 40 at the main entrance of the Painted Desert. The Petrified Forest awaited on the far south end of the park. We spent an entire day stopping at the various outlooks, taking the hikes, and peeling our dropped jaws off the ground. If rocks ate LSD, they'd produce this kind of psychedelic landscape. The hikes were astounding in the initial stretches of the Painted Desert and only got better inside the Petrified Forest.

The Petrified Forest was a mind-blower. Giant logs made of multicolored stone dazzled us with spectacular color variations and textures. I could spend hours staring at any one of the massive stone trees we saw.

On the far end, in a gem store parking lot, there is free boondocking. For ten bucks, which we paid, you get electricity. In that big parking lot, there were so many dropped minerals, I didn't need to buy any. It is illegal to take shards of petrified wood from the park, but you can buy some at the store or find it in the parking lot.

After time spent in stone forests, we made our way back through the park, enjoying another leisurely day. Every vista was too fantastic to drive past. There aren't any words to describe it. This will remain one of our all-time favorite places.

Lisa's Tale: Breakdown After Canyon De Chelly Email

We left Canyon De Chelly (pronounced De-shay) heading for the vast nothingness that surrounds Natural Bridges, Arches National Park, Bryce Canyon, etc. There appears from the map to be no real significant towns in this part of Utah.

Partway on our journey, we happened to notice that our alternator was not charging. Luckily, we had not traveled past civilization by too much and were within about 100 miles of a town. We were able to limp into Farmington, N.M., near the Four Corners area. It was one of two places on the map that looked to have the services we needed, like repair shops and auto parts stores.

After removing the alternator and replacing it with another in the parking lot of the auto parts store (in Farmington), we restarted the engine only to find that we were still not charging. Since this is a dual battery system and has additional components not found on a car, I was a bit stumped. We stayed in the auto parts parking lot for the night to seek out a repair shop in the morning.

Turns out not only do we need a voltage regulator, but we also need the pigtail (wire do-hickey thing) to it. The repair shop had the regulator but had to order the pigtail, so we are here another night. This time, we are in a campground where we have electricity and can make use of our amenities. Amazing how much you appreciate the little things after not having them (lights, water pump, etc.).

Hopefully, the part will arrive as scheduled, the repair will be effective as expected, and we can continue on our way. We sure were lucky to discover the problem before we got away from help!

~ Lisa

Rachel's Tale: Canyon De Chelly and UFOs in New Mexico

March 19, 2011 (Written while waiting for parts in Farmington, N.M.)

After the Petrified Forest, the Canyon De Chelly, a Federal Park on the Navajo reservation in Arizona, was our next tourist stop and campsite. The camping is free so we went. That was a mistake. The water didn't work and the vagabonds were a pain in the ass.

At night, after the park rangers were off-site. Every night, a number of Native Americans selling artwork knocked on our door. We witnessed a steady stream of locals coming into the campground to try and get free water and use the bathrooms. Of course, the water wasn't working.

We had to fill up our tanks the hard way on the way out—by buying water at the local food market one gallon at a time with refilled bottles. It took about 25 gallons at 25 cents a gallon. What sucked was a drunk man kept begging us for money as we slowly filled the tanks. It took many trips in and out of the store. I finally gave the guy a buck so he'd leave us alone, but he waited for us at the door on our next trip to beg for more. I turned around and went back into the store and asked management to have an employee escort us out. These sad human circumstances almost outstripped the staggering natural beauty we witnessed.

Getting back to the good stuff.

We drove the south rim, a very nice 32-mile round trip with about six pull-over locations to see the glory of the Canyon De Chelly. Frankly, the views were staggering. Each pull-off presented a weird dichotomy as persistent Native American hawkers worked every parking lot. They sold Native American art objects from paintings of the petroglyphs to jewelry.

The canyon floor and cannon cliffs held adobe ruins of pueblos, or cliff dwellings. The drop

From the website, about the ruins:
You can either cross the bridge or simply walk downstream (if there is no water) until you see White House Ruin on the right at the base of the cliff. Navajo vendors selling arts and crafts are frequently sitting quietly in the shade of the trees beside the stream.

The light-colored plaster on some of the rooms led to the Navajo name for the site—*Kinii' ni gai*—which means White House. Archaeologists believe the rooms on the canyon floor used to be high enough to provide access to the upper rooms in the alcove.

Although people have lived in Canyon de Chelly for more than 5,000 years, it was Ancestral Puebloans who built White House around 1060 AD. More rooms were added during the next 200 years, and archaeologists estimate there may have been up to 80 rooms and four kivas when it was most heavily used.[1]

---

1   https://www.grandcanyontrust.org/hikes/cpe-white-house-ruin

averaged 700 feet. We took the mile-and-a-half hike down a crazy switch-backed path to the White House Native American ruins. It was a fantastic overlook and a challenging hike.

What else did we find at the ruins?

Native American hawkers, of course. Native Americans are persistent at the hard-sell. The history of Native oppression and their poverty make it hard to say no, especially when they tell you they want to earn a dollar to buy a potato for dinner.

Near the end of the day, we made it to the last pull-over at Spider Rock. I could have marveled at it for hours but it was getting late. A pregnant hawker, her husband, and mother-in-law convinced us to give them a ride to the campground where we were staying. The pregnant girl asked us for a beer. Once at the campground, they sat on our picnic table until dark. Then, they knocked on every camper's door trying to sell their art. They knocked on our door, too. They made us a great deal, ten bucks for a petroglyph painting on a piece of flat sandstone.

We already had one, but we bought it anyway.

After all, they needed food (or maybe beer). The farther we got from the campground, the cheaper the art we saw cost. By the time we hit the outskirts of town, earrings we had seen for fifteen dollars were now two bucks a pair. After getting water, we left the reservation town going north on 191 and drove 60 miles through the Navajo landscape on our way to Moab, Utah.

Wild horses and dogs were evident everywhere.

We didn't reach it…yet.

Along the road, we discovered an electrical problem with the truck and changed course midstream to limp back into New Mexico heading for the nearest big town, Farmington, N.M., where parts were available. Farmington is 100 miles from the reservation, and we were lucky to make it. We were running on a dead battery, so we could not shut the motor off and had to drive until we got there.

Once in town, we went to an auto parts store and got a new alternator. The one we had was new a year ago. Turns out the alternator was not the problem. So, we wasted 60 bucks installing a part in a parking lot that we didn't need. Nice of the parts store people to let us sleep in their parking lot though.

The next morning, we were lucky to get an appointment at a place that could test it. They found the problem. In older cars, the voltage regulator is not built into the alternator—a fact Lisa and I both knew, but forgot since all newer cars have both components integrated.

We were forced to camp in a place that wasn't cheap, buy parts we didn't need, pay a guy to fix it when we could have done it ourselves (had we remembered), in a town we never planned to visit. At least, the car shop guy figured out the pigtail wire was bad, or we would not have known that. They ordered the part. So, now I'm sitting at the shop, been

here all day, and waiting for a guy to go to
the junkyard. They do have a regulator.

A five-minute job takes two days.

All is not bad, let's talk about the good side.

The ride up 191 above I-40 and then the
ride on our alternate routes, 491 and 64 into
Farmington were fantastic. The campground here
in Farmington has a great, nice hot shower
and I finally shaved my legs after 3 weeks of
growth! The mechanic found problems we didn't
know about and that is super good. Those
issues are being addressed as I write this.

Due to the diverted route, we are now
going to go to Mesa Verde in southern central
Colorado, which wasn't part of our original
plan. It looks like a fantastic place,
hopefully without Native hawkers or camping
fees. There is a cheap, paid campground near
it. We will stock up on free water and cheaper
supplies while here in Farmington.

Did I mention that the food prices on the
reservation were criminally high?

It seems the white man is still fucking the
Indians.

Another boon I must mention: The manager
of this car repair place (Wes) had a fantastic
tale to share about a UFO sighting. He brought
in the original photos his friends took of a
UFO using an old Kodak Instamatic 110 camera,
complete with a date stamp from 1974. You
can't fake this kind of film. This turned out
to be the best-looking UFO pictures I've seen,
barring Billy Meier's pictures.[10] Wes' pictures
have never been published. They have a record
of the film's development as well. This looks

---

10   From the Sotheby's website when they auctioned off the photos: Taken in
1975 by "Billy" Eduard Albert Meier, alleged extraterrestrial contactee and the
founder of Freie Interessengemeinschaft für Grenz- und Geisteswissenschafter und
Geisteswissenschafter und Ufologiestudien (Free Community of Interests for the
Border and Spiritual Sciences and Ufological Studies), these images purport to depict
an interstellar visit by spacecraft from the planet Erra, two with a single UFO moving slowly over the town of Berg Rumlikon, in Switzerland on June 14, 1975 at 1:16 and
1:20 pm, and four images depicting a single UFO in a forested hilly area of Schmidrüti,
Switzerland on March 18th, 1975, from 4:45 to 5:40 pm."

like the real deal. I implored the guy to
write up the story and submit it to the Mutual
UFO Network, AKA, MUFON.

Here is Wes' short version of the UFO story
I'll paraphrase:

A family friend who was in his 20s in
1974 and his wife were at a local spring
with a metal detector looking for Spanish
conquistador armor. The Spaniards were known
to have traveled this far north into New
Mexico. The couple had the camera on them
with three pictures left on the roll. The
UFO appeared, and the guy started shooting.
They finished the roll and loaded a new roll.
The first roll, the one with only three UFO
pictures on it, was tossed into the car's glove
compartment and forgotten.

The UFO circled the couple's position about
50 to 100 yards out as if doing a survey.
All the while, Wes' mother's friends shot the
entire second roll of film. Then, they went
directly to the drug store and had the film
developed. They did not remember the roll in
the glove compartment.

They showed the pictures to people in town.
Finally, pictures in hand, they called federal
officials. Two guys showed up, one in a black
suit and the other in a United States Air
Force uniform. These government representatives
warned the couple not to talk. They also
confiscated the pictures and negatives. When
the photographers asked for copies, the couple
were told to shut up. The government men left
without leaving their names.

The officials never returned. Everyone was
scared shitless.

A few weeks later, the family discovered
the first roll of film in the glove box. When
they got it developed, they found typical
family photos and three very good UFO shots.
One shot shows the object standing on end.
One shot shows it rising and split at the

center to reveal a row of windows. The final shot shows the UFO straight on. All the shots are near trees, so it is easy to see the size and shape by contrast. Very sharp and clear photos. The old photographs were tattered from age around the edges but fine other than that.

The guy who took the pictures has since died, but his wife is still alive as I write this.

How did Wes get the pictures?

It was like this: when the guy found more pictures, he didn't know what to do. He wanted to turn them over to the federal government. He thought it was illegal to have them.

Wes's mom piped up. Wes was about five-years-old at the time, but he remembered.

"I'll take the pictures," she said. "I'm not scared."

The rest is family lore.

I told Wes to get the wife's statement before she died. Then, he should send the pictures and a detailed story to the Mutual UFO Network (MUFON). Wes said he would ask the women to make a signed statement.

I've read 50-some books over the years on UFOs. I've seen similar photos. Some very famous pictures are of the same craft. To see undocumented originals with a plausible story was another occasion to have my mind blown. This diversion was a great thing—I finally got to see a UFO picture that was not in a book. Far out!

By the way, Wes' sister owns the furniture store across the street from the Roswell Museum. Small world, or small universe, as the case may be.

~Rachel[11]

---

11 By the way, I am not convinced UFOs are aliens. Pictures and stories are not hard evidence. I don't know what they are and neither does anyone else. I have yet to see testable, repeatable evidence to prove anything.

Finding Mesa Verde

March 21, 2011 from email:

I don't know if I'm an optimist in the emotional sense, but I am an optimist in the intellectual sense. Even in the middle of a river of bad shit, I always stone-step on solid turds.

It is not luck. We look for opportunities as a force of habit, and so we find them.

Make the bad into good. Problems become boons.

So how does that ideal comply with Lisa and Rachel's great adventure?

"What was so great about the on-the-road electrical problems you had? Didn't you go out of your way for repairs?"

That is true. However, examine this silver lining. If we did not notice the problem early, we would have been stranded on the side of a road in the middle of nowhere. Furthermore, if it were not for bailing, we would not have gone to Mesa Verde.

Mesa Verde was a pinnacle visit, but there were little advantages to be had right from the words, "We might have a problem here." By going off course, we had the opportunity to witness views of landscape we would not have otherwise seen. The road out of Farmington, New Mexico, into Colorado was spectacular. The landscape again changed radically—from high desert to the Pineland Mountains' high ranges. What a great trip!

Getting stuck in Farmington for three days was an actual pleasure. We managed to correct an earlier repair we made that was done wrong. Thus, we prevented future problems. We got everything we needed. Then, there was Ma and Pa's RV Park. That's its real name. I rant a lot about the lack of ma-and-pa operations in the United States due to corporate displacement, and here a real ma-and-pa place restored my hope for small enterprise.

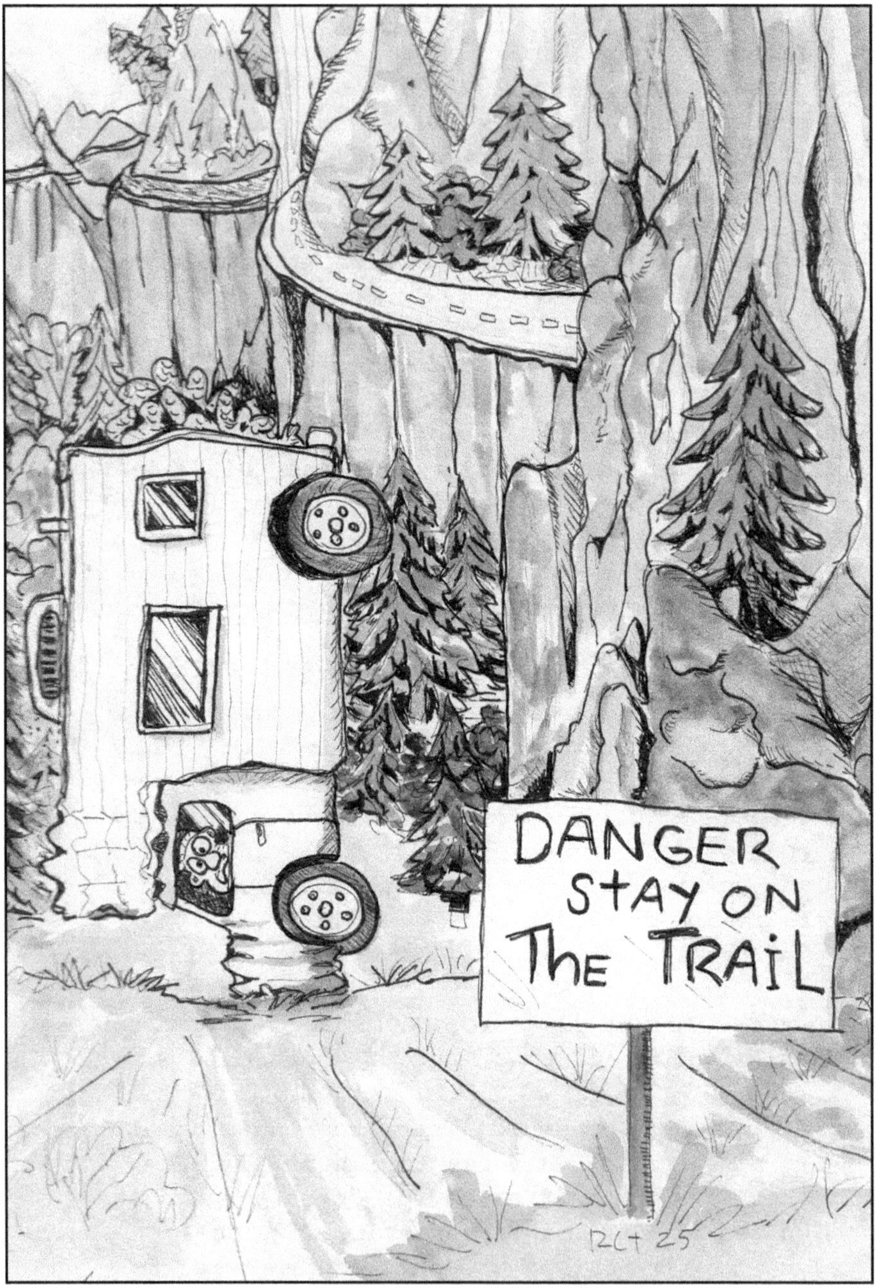
DANGER
stay ON
The TRAiL
RCT 25

Ma and Pa had the usual things we crave but
seldom get such as:

It was easy to find.

It was easy to park.

Full hookups.

Great clean showers with lots of hot water.

Quiet neighbors.

Ma and Pa hit every mark, but that wasn't the
best part.[12] Pa had a toy shop and a huge outdoor
train set. He makes toys of all sorts for train
sets of all sizes and sells them. Collectors
and builders know his name. He makes everything
from little tiny people to German toy soldier
sets, landscape items, even complete towns
and factories in miniature. He works in all
materials, but he is also one of the few people
who paint metal figurines the old-fashioned 19th
century way. This was yet another small and
unexpected museum along the road.

Driving out, we finally found New Mexico's
middle class. Away from reservation lands,
people seemed to be doing all right. They had
nicer homes, pets, non-work horses, and RVs
in the driveway—RVs that were not the primary
residence. In short, there was less abject
poverty going north out of Farmington.

I saw lots of junk in yards; junk always
interests me—there could be treasures in
there. But here, these were not piles of rust-
rotting scrap metal stacked around desperate
homes. These junk collections were supplies
for serious hobbyists and professional car
restorers. We saw a lot of rusted but usable
antique cars from the 1920s to the 1960s. I got
the feeling this land was a regional rescue
mission for old cars from the South.

In the dry conditions of the Southwest,
cars left in the elements last a long, long
time. In the wet South, they rot apart fast. I
also noticed lots of antique farm tractors and

---

12   Research suggests that Ma and Pa might be deceased now and that the park and
museum are no longer in operation.

equipment. One yard in Colorado boasted dozens of rare tractors.

Special things you find on the road are not always things, sometimes they are people. We stopped in a roadside combination post office, gas station, general store and newsstand in Colorado somewhere along Route 64 heading northwest. We met the very nice owner, an old hippie chick of our vein, a real child of the 60s. She was about my age, nice to talk with, shared lots of info on the area, and she had a good story to tell. Her dad had a much-coveted-by-collectors 1938 Indian motorcycle in original condition and good running order. When he died, her mother gave it to a stranger. It was worth more than $100,000. As an antique motorcycle geek, I hated hearing a story of that kind. What a sad loss.

There is a cosmic lesson here. Look for the stepping stones in the river of trouble and you'll get to the other side.

I'm on top of a mesa right now at the Natural Bridges National Monument, Utah, campground, 37 miles from the nearest highway, Route 191. I'm getting caught up writing about our recent adventures emails for when we get Internet again. It was snowing when we arrived. The road was steep and tricky with lots of switchbacks. We'll need to stay until the snow melts.

I'm not worried. More to come about this place in another email.

~ Rachel

On Top of Mesa Verde

March 24, 2011 email:

The ride to Mesa Verde through Colorado was incredible. The scenery was vast and quite different from New Mexico. As we drove, we saw distant snow-covered peaks that kept getting closer.

"Gee, I hope we don't have to drive over them," we said.

Guess what? We had to.

We hit elevations of more than 8,500 feet with snow all around us. It did not look good.

Thankfully, once we topped the high ground, we had a long downward drive to Mesa Verde Park. Once in the deep valley, there was little or no snow. The weather turned foul and foggy with distant snow or rain all around us soon after we entered the park.

We didn't know what we were getting into.

The road into Mesa Verde is 20 miles long, twisted, and nothing but sharply up and down. It was hard to see, but at least the road was dry. Steep grades, switchbacks, and 180-degree hairpin turns (without guardrails) ran along cliff edges. I had to drive 15 miles-per-hour on some hills with the truck in first gear. Lisa was white. I was tense. But we made it.

It was worth it.

We got there early. The weather had cleared before arrival. Once on top of the mesa, it was a wonderland: a dwarf forest of pinyon pines, ponderosa pine, juniper, aspen, and weird white-skinned oaks. Along the road, we stopped to photograph wild horses and noticed mule deer right next to the road. Four yearling deer played while an older doe stood nearby.

The visitor's center offered another excellent museum with Native American artifacts, fossils, geological displays, and much more. The museum itself is a destination worthy of a day trip.

Behind the visitor's center was a path leading us on a quarter mile descent to the canyon's bottom, and then, a few hundred feet up the other side of the riff to Native American cliff dwellings. Not only did we get close to the ruins, but we were allowed inside them…to a point. This was a first. All the substantial ruins we saw so far were at a distance or strictly hands-off when allowed near them. Look, but don't touch!

In Canyon De Chelly, we had hiked 1.5 miles one-way on a difficult path only to see the ruins from behind a fence 200 yards away. Here we were right inside them and the only visitors, except for one guy talking to the ranger. Mr. Ranger allowed us to enter a kiva[13] and to walk inside the ruins.[14]

After that, we drove one of the two mesa top loops with pull-offs to view many more ruins and off-the-hook canyon views. The many ruins we saw were pretty darn close. These Native Americans built their homes near the top of the mesa rather than the bottom. The idea was to make their pueblo inaccessible to enemies.

| **TIP:** The views in Mesa Verde allow visitors to collect great photographs without extreme telephoto capabilities but if you have zoom lenses bring them.

After the driving tour, we were exhausted and happy. It was getting late. Perhaps we

---

13   For more information on kivas and southwestern archaeology read *When Is A Kiva*, by Watson Smith; ISBN 978-0816511556

14   From the National Park Service website: Kiva is a Hopi word. At Mesa Verde, they were often round, underground rooms and tended to be small household kivas that were used for a mix of routine and special purposes such as a place to hold ceremonies. Notice the small hole near the fire pit? This is the Sipapu, a Hopi word for "place of emergence." According to Hopi oral tradition, this hole represents the place where Ancestral Pueblo people emerged from the previous world to this one. Much like the biblical story of Noah's Ark, Hopis believe that the world before this one was destroyed, but a few chosen people were saved. Climbing a ladder up out of the smoky kiva and through the roof into the courtyard after ceremonies may have served as a powerful reminder of their movement from the world before. In pueblo villages today, kivas have special uses and meanings. It appears that every clan (made up of the extended family) had its own kiva for use during ceremonies and other social events. https://tinyurl.com/bd83ym3n

could have done the other loop too, but we had
had our fill. Later in the season, people can
climb into a variety of the ruins. Mesa Verde,
like the Petrified Forest, should not be seen
in only one day.

In a bittersweet development, a recent
forest fire exposed more than 600 "new" ruins.
As a result, Mesa Verde National Park can only
get better. We will go to Mesa Verde again,
and when we do, we hope to spend days walking
in the footprints of the Hopi Native American
tribes.

This was our best stop to-date for exploring
Native American ruins. And we never would have
gone if it weren't for car trouble.

Sometimes it's good when cars take a dump.

Another good thing about going to Mesa
Verde was the driving practice for our next
stop: Natural Bridges National Monument, Utah,
where the access road was twice as long, more
difficult, and even steeper.

Mesa Verde was, in all, a huge boon.

~ Rachel

Natural Bridges and a Tricky Entrance

March 24, 2011 email:

One thing I haven't mentioned much in my emails is the problem of hills.

It turns out that hills suck.

I mean, who would know that?

I'm driving a 1978 truck that was not designed to climb steep hills. I'm towing a trailer with an extra 1000 pounds of momentum (mass). That is to say another 1000 pounds of drag-anchor or can't-stop depending on if one is going uphill or downhill. This trailer doesn't have brakes. More mass means more stress on the truck's brakes making it harder to stop even though we are within its tow capacity limits.

We have been over all kinds of twisty-turned mountains. I even overheated the brakes once in Virgina. Every twisty mountain road scares the shit out of me, but going into Natural Bridges took the cake being the worst road yet. Mesa Verde had the bad-road prize locked up until we got here. The grades around Natural Bridges were the steepest of any I've seen.

A six-percent grade is the norm for a steep road. These hills go up and down at eight-percent (perhaps a little more?) for a distance of 37 miles. I needed to drive very, very slow downhill with the transmission in low gear so I didn't build up speed a lot.

Maybe the cold fog and low temperatures helped keep the brakes cool. My advice? Do not overheat the brakes at all costs, brake fade is scary.

Uphill at 7,000 feet, there is a lack of carburetor air which compounded the difficulties along with the eight-percent grade. In practice, where possible, I started at the top of a hill and accelerated to 55 miles per hour or even 60 on the way down and was lucky to make 25 miles per hour by the time I crested the next hill.

Thirty-seven miles of this crap in between
dead slow downhills to get to Natural Bridges.
Scary!

It was worth it. Even if 37 miles did take
more than two hours.

Natural Bridges is one of those federal
parks with a size limit of 25-feet on a site.
We were towing a motorcycle trailer. The
trailer put us over the limit. No problem, we
parked the trailer in the parking lot of the
visitor's complex ranger station, gift shop,
and educational center.

Once we got in, very late for us at 3 p.m.,
all we had time for was setting up camp. We
took a campsite for two days thinking we'd
see the park the next day and leave the
morning after. Our site at Natural Bridges
was enchanting. Situated on high, flat ground
which might have been a mesa. This ground
was surrounded by canyons with trails to the
bottom. Fantastic scenery! On that first night,
it snowed.

Yeah, I know we took off to avoid the snow
last year. But the alternative in this area
is scorching heat. It's better to experience
the high desert in early spring or late fall,
and in some cases, winter is the best time to
visit.

We were lucky so far, always just ahead
of or behind bad weather. That first night in
Natural Bridges, besides snowing, got down to
27 degrees. It seemed our luck ran out.

We were prepared: well-stocked with propane,
food, and clothes. We woke up to a snow-
covered camper and trees, but the ground was
sun-warmed and the snow didn't stick. Thank
the Goddess! How lucky were we? It turned into
a beautiful day.

We took the driving tour, a nine-mile
loop, on motorcycles. This high ground was
surrounded by canyons with trails to the
bottom. Fantastic scenery! Canyon or topside,

the hiking trails were great! Trails from easy
to hardcore were available. We hiked down to
one of the Natural Bridges, 500 feet below
the overlook at the canyon's bottom. It was a
tough, steep hike, but safe as the trail was
clear of snow. The view of the natural bridge
from the bottom of the canyon was simply
priceless, and the area had very cool flora
with an oak tree patch besides. The underside
of the natural bridge stood 50 feet above us.
We dressed warmly, and frankly, I'd rather do
this in the cold than in the hot. It was a
perfect day.

That night, magic happened. It was cold,
true, but the sky was a mind-blower. Stars
were out in force. The sky watching here is
the best in the United States. I never saw
so many stars so well. The best scenery here
has to be the night sky with its staggering
clarity. Natural Bridges is known as the
darkest sky in America. Amazing how the sky
looks without ambient light anywhere.

The ranger station has a couple of
refracting telescopes on wheels for summer
programs. They wheel them out to sight stars

and then project the telescope's reading onto a wall in the amphitheater. But I didn't need a telescope to enjoy this night sky. It was so good I put my binoculars away. You just haven't seen the night sky until you have seen it in the high desert!

Oddly, we started this trip with warm-weather camping in mind and have been doing cold-weather camping ever since we left Pennsylvania for the second time last fall. But it's been all good. We keep missing the worst of the weather and benefiting from the fact that very few people are out here with us. We have a lot of places all to ourselves.

I guess some people know about this secret because Natural Bridges had a fair amount of people—not a crowd—not enough to mess with our bliss, just enough people around so that if we needed help, we could get it. Next month, this and other National Parks will be crazy. It's good to stay ahead of the people-wave.

The drive out was not bad. Okay, I lied. The drive was white-knuckled, but at least we were on the side of the road with a lesser need for guardrails. Most of the sheer cliff drop-offs were on the uphill side.

~ Rachel

Moab, Arches and Horse Thief Campground

March 27, 2011 email:

What we needed after Natural Bridges was a place to dump our waste tanks, get a long overdue shower, wash a pile of clothes, and fill up on water. Therefore, we landed five miles below the town of Moab, Utah. Moab is eight miles below Arches National Park. We pulled into a campground called OK RV Park.[15]

You don't know how good a hot shower is until you have not had one in five days. However, at first, we did not start out happy. The Passport America discount price was higher than listed on the web and in the literature. But that top-shelf shower and laundromat fixed our disdain.

Amazing how a good shower and clean clothes can wash away petty concerns. $17.50 a night is more than we like to pay, but the other campgrounds were 40 bucks. We stayed three nights and enjoyed some free cable TV and Internet. I got my travel logs up to date and emailed them out. I wrote another killer chapter for my new book. It's been hard to sit down and write.

The next stop was supposed to be Arches, but we found out that the federal campground inside the park was booked *for the season*—WTF!

So, while at OK RV, we came up with an alternative plan. We found a Bureau of Land Management campground less than 20 miles from Arches. God bless the Bureau of Land Management—they have camps cheap or free all over the place. While the other campers pack into the well-known National Parks, we get these other great places to ourselves. We broke camp in the morning and off we went planning to tour Arches. We had plenty of time, or so we thought.

---

15   To see another camper's video review of OK RV Park: https://www.youtube.com/watch?v=SxfzLGCSF2E&t=153s

Not two miles from OK RV, I pulled into a gas station (not the cheaper one I was told of and forgot about) and discovered we had a gas leak!

Shit! What now?

The fuel pump was toast.

Of course, it could not have broken while we were sitting in a nice, comfortable campground waiting for the weather. That would be too easy. It had to bust in a parking lot.

"Let's look at the bright side," I said to Lisa.

Lisa didn't want to hear it, but it could have been much worse. The truck could have burned, or we may not have noticed the fuel pump malfunction until all of our gas had poured out onto the highway.

The guy we got the truck from had given us a new fuel pump. He never installed it. I had it in the box. We had the truck running again in an hour. (This is a mechanical pump that is attached to the motor unlike new trucks which have the pump inside the gas tank.) We felt so good that we decided to get a bite to eat on our way to tour Arches. Money was tight—but what the hell, we saved our asses yet again! The looks we got in the parking lot were priceless.

Driving into the town of Moab was cool. It's a tourist trap town but nice, very active in the old nature-hippie sort of way, a breath of fresh air. However, Moab was also inundated with dirt bikers, mountain bikers, and jeep rental places (for off-road tours) between the town's cool little shops. I learned that Moab is the only hippie liberal bastion in the state of Utah.

We had quiche, and it was good!

After a nice but pricey lunch, Lisa realized she had lost her keys. So, we retraced our steps. They weren't at the bike shop where we bought chain lube, or fossil store. They weren't at the gas station or gift shop. We headed back to the campground with little hope. Near the entrance, I saw her keys on the side of the road. Salvation! A few keys were damaged, but the important ones survived. We had spares for the rest. Never go anywhere without spare keys!

Finally, off to Arches. We were not in a very good mood and it was getting late. We decided to do a quick tour, check it out, and return after the weekend when the tourists had gone. We dropped the trailer in the visitor center's parking lot. Leaving the motorcycles on the trailer in the parking lot meant we'd have better brakes and use less gas.

We didn't drive one mile into the park when the trials of the day were forgotten due to the scenery around us. The farther we drove, the more astounded we became. We babbled words and phrases like surreal, inconceivable, astounding, mind-bending, and, "I think I'm tripping" and "That can't be real."

Before dark, we decided to get to the campground and set up at the Bureau of Land Management site called Horse Thief. The day after setting up, Sunday, was spent doing camper maintenance stuff, setting up our solar panels, and running the generator which had been idle for months.

If the weather improves, we will set out early and do Arches the way it should be done, long, slow, and with quiet reverence. You see, on the weekend, Arches is crazy with obnoxious people who drive fast and crazy. I don't know why anyone would come all the way out here into this fantastic wilderness just to race up and down the mesa like they were late for work.

Arches is a high desert wonderland of more than 2000 stone arches, crazy rock outcrops, and amazing landscape formations. The road to the campground, which is found at the back end of the park, is a slow 18-miles long

Expect the unexpected.

meandering ride from the park's entrance. This,
the only road, holds many pull-over vistas and
hiking trails along the way.

We spent three nights in Horse Thief.
We were low on money, and it was cheap. It
was the kind of place we like, quiet and
deserted. (For anyone following our path keep
this in mind: no utilities, only pit toilets,
and large, level camp lots.) We didn't get
to ride the bikes as we planned because the
weather was too cold. The views were good. We
hiked the local trail, and I spent half a day
going from campsite to campsite searching for
abandoned firewood.

Remember deadfall is usually fair game, but
in certain national parks and federal lands,
there is no gathering of local wood permitted
at all. It's an environmental preservation
thing. There is good dead wood around like
pinion pine, long-burning juniper, and
ponderosa but there isn't enough. Campers would
clean the place out inside a year if they
were allowed to take wood. You got to bring
your own wood here. That's right, BYOW. Most
national forests are just the opposite—you

can't BYOW as a countermeasure to tree diseases and tree-eating bug infestations. It is easier to scavenge than it is to gather in either case.

Lisa calls me the fire woman. I take my fires seriously, and I lovingly tend them. I'm good at wood cutting, splitting, starting, and keeping the fire. I always find good stuff to burn. At Horse Thief, finding wood was a challenge. The rule here is to burn your fires down to ash and do not use sand to extinguish them. As I walked the place, I noticed human footprints and ATV tracks which suggested that the camp host also raids the place for leftovers daily. Never fear, Rachel had success.

I took the stuff that Mr. Camp Host wouldn't touch. I gathered up all the burnt wood. You know, what they used to call charcoal. I can give you the entire history of charcoal, from its origins to its ancient and modern uses and methods of making it. Perhaps another time. The Navajo Indians here still make and sell charcoal. I got the gourmet stuff for free. Natural charcoal is the best for barbeque or any other open-fire cooking in our opinion.

That night, we ate the best campfire-cooked burgers you can imagine. We took a couple of fresh onions and a can of mushrooms and fried them with a little wine. It was a killer burger-topping. Eating well is a huge boon while roughing it.

We broke camp early and headed into Arches. The weather had improved. The sky was clear, and it was warm, a perfect day in many ways. There were fewer tourists. We even managed to get a campsite inside the park, almost impossible to do on short notice.

"How'd you do that?"

At the park entrance, the ranger said there was a cancellation. He warned us that it was not guaranteed. The campground is at the end

of the park, 18 miles from the gate. Only
the camp host would know for sure about the
cancellation. Normally, I would not try it.
This time, we figured we'd go all the way to
the end and work our way out. Nothing to lose.

We got to the camp host, only to find there
were no vacancies. However, the only sites
that can't be reserved are the handicapped-
accessible sites, and one was unoccupied.

I have a handicapped placard. I have it
for a reason, but I seldom use it. I figure
there are people more in need than I am in
the average Walgreens' parking lot. But out
here—screw it! We took that site for a night.

So, as I said this park requires a long,
slow look. The more I walk, the worse I feel.
I often put the pain aside and feel it later.
Now, after a day exploring, I'm satisfied, but
I am in need of this campsite because I can
hardly walk. The site is level, wide, and near
the restroom. Why do I always feel like a
cheater when I use my handicapped placard?

The next day, after Lisa and I broke
camp, we toured our missed Arches' points
of interest. Lisa and I agreed that as
overwhelming as it was, Arches wasn't our
favorite stop. The Petrified Forest and Three
Rivers were better.

In Bureau of Land Management camps and
other remote places, most people respect
nature and each other. These campers are not
tourists. They are real campers. They know how
not to destroy things.

In Arches, people come from California and
other distant places. They come like a swarm
of locusts on spring break. They drive through
the park well past the speed limit. They
would pass me on a curve just to stop at the
next pull-over to take pictures. They'll park
anyplace, cut you off, and tailgate.

We hiked many paths. Everyone is marked
with signs that say, "Stay on the trail" or

"This is not a trail." Yet people's footprints go off in every direction. No respect for the park, nature, or the future pristine condition of the park for others to enjoy and for science to study. And everywhere we saw garbage.

"People suck," Lisa and I told each other.

You can take a person out of civilization, but you can't civilize them. Why do people come to wild parks and act like animals? I find nothing civil about civilized man.

Only deeply connected nature loving campers seem to get it.

My advice is: Avoid great big national parks where clueless people roam without any concept or respect for the sacredness of nature.

Go where people who "get it" go. They step off their treadmill before arriving on site. At the primitive places off the beaten path, that is where you will find civilized people.

Bryce Canyon is still reported to be snowed-in, so the next stop is Zion (another big National Park) or Las Vegas, two equally uncivilized places, I'm sure.

~ Rachel

Next stop: Zion National Park, Utah (300 miles away)

April 6, 2011 email:

Day One

We came to Zion as the north side of the
Grand Canyon was still closed due to snow. The
name Zion is an old Hebrew word that means
sanctuary or a place of rest. Good name,
although we have not rested much. It looks
restful, but there's too much to see to kick
back. We booked our site for four nights. Our
last Walmart boondock was only 40 miles from
here so we arrived early, set up, and had time
to check things out.

Here in Zion, they eliminated the
destructive forces of car traffic in the park.
That is good as more than three million
people a year come here. You know how clueless
and stupid people can be. At first, I was a
little pissed because I couldn't drive where
I wanted. I hate being tightly-controlled by
the government. I hate tourist traps. This
certainly is one.

I've since changed my mind, in this case.
This no-drive situation is much better for the
health of the park. That's what matters most to
Lisa and I.

So how does one get around in Zion?

Why, the new, clean propane-powered buses
that run every ten minutes, of course. The bus
is free and it takes you into and out of the
deepest reaches of the upper canyon bottom.
There are many stops. Each has one or more
trails. The information guides posted at each
trail head, and in brochures, are excellent so
one can decide what hike and at what difficulty
level one feels confident in trying.

The visitor's center is designed for the
massive volume of people that come here. So
is the Lodge. The museum, with its how-to-do-
the-park movie every 20 minutes, also helps
control the clueless. Right outside the front

gate is the town of Springfield. Springfield offers a mile and a half of quaint little shops with lots of crappy food places in between retail stores. This free bus also takes people out of the park and into town away from us.

Lisa and I took the bus upstream so we could get an idea of the layout. At the end, we did the three-mile round-trip hike along the Virgin River. In most canyon parks we noticed the main features and facilities are along the canyon rims with hiking trails down into the canyons. Here, everything happens at the bottom of the canyon. The hikes take you up to the roadless rim or along the Virgin River running swiftly from north to south. That's different and cool.

Life on the floor of the canyon is spectacular. Cottonwood trees were so lime green my eyes hurt. Spring had sprung at the bottom of the canyon along the river but not up on the rim. It was 75 degrees with an intensely hot sun.

Just two days before, 100 miles north as the crow flies, and 3,000 feet higher, we had snow. Road travel between Arches and Zion is 300 miles.

The bus tour recording says that the temperature differences cause radical environmental changes between the top and the bottom of the canyon. The elevation differential creates "micro-environments." I love that. Two for the price of one is a good thing.

Day Two
Hot and sunny. In the morning, we took a hike to the canyon rim. It was a trip and not for the reasons you'd think. The trail was steep and hard. Near the top, the trail was narrow and steeper still with sheer drops to certain death if you faltered. Very dangerous. The trails guide warned that this hike was not recommended for children and people fearful of

heights, and for good reason! You don't want to trip here.

But the real "trip" was the number of dumb-ass people on the trail without proper gear, shoes, or water, and some folks with kids in tow! A few parents hiked with babies strapped on their backs. How do you change a diaper on a ledge 500 feet up? They must have ignored the warning signs.

People can be stupid.

Every park should require people to read, *actually* read, the warnings before entry. One such warning says that people fall and die every year in this park. However, I guess these family units don't read anything more challenging than Dr. Seuss! Everyone receives a copy of the rules at the gate. You can lead a horse to water…Oh, never mind.

Afternoon. The weather is fantastically warm even in higher elevations. We jumped on the motorcycles and took Utah State Route 9 which runs in and out of Zion. The buses don't go there. Anyone can drive it after paying to get into the park unless they have the Federal Access Pass then entry is free. It is a highway and not a park road. This was a fantastic 12-mile ride to the top of the mesa and on to the park's rear gate. We didn't go farther, but Route 9 continues. We saw the top of Zion up close. That includes traversing a 1.2-mile tunnel. On the far side of the tunnel, it was a completely different world with snow in shady places.

This may have been one of the best motorcycle rides of my life. It took us four hours for the 24-mile round trip. Our little dirt bikes were great for the steep, twisty climbs and descents. Lisa, with her fear of heights, and the lack of guard rails made our return downhill ride very slow, but that's just fine—more to see.

Day Three

The park info guide tells of sudden and drastic weather changes. So, as usual, we stocked our hiking pack with just-in-case-gear. We headed for a hike to the Emerald Pools. Halfway up it started to rain a little.

No problem, we had rain gear so on we went. The family in front of us—four kids, a dad, and a pregnant wife all in T-shirts—raced ahead trying to beat the rain. It was a steep, wet, slippery climb. We made it to the top warm, dry, and safe. That under-dressed family who passed us on the way up came back down before we reached the pool. After they passed us again, we carefully continued the climb. Most of the people on that climb were ill-prepared which was a boon for us. By the time we reached the spectacular upper pool, the herd had thinned considerably. We had the place nearly to ourselves, except for a few smart people with the right gear. The hike down was quiet and peaceful.

Day Four

We woke to cloudy skies and cold weather. The temperature had dropped 40 degrees since day one. The ranger report said there is a 50 percent chance of rain. We are so damn lucky. Why is it lucky?

Because the bad forecast made most people go home or stay in. Most, but not all. We played our cards safe and decided on the Watchmen Hike, well equipped, of course, a hike that started at the campground. 50 yards down the road, a young couple with two small kids were at the river's edge playing in the sand before we started the hike.

That is incredibly dumb. Let me explain. The Virgin River is fast, deep, and powerful. It drops, on average, 71 feet per mile. That's very, very fast and very dangerous. Any kid

that falls into that flow rate will disappear
forever.

This river is full of rocks and debris.
Only a year ago, a flash flood wiped out a park
road. Right now, is flash flood season. With
yesterday's slight rain, the river is high and
faster than the day before. There are storms
up river, too. That makes perfect conditions
for flash floods.

Back to the hike…It was great because, as
I said, hardly anyone was on the trail. We got
to see yet another perspective of the park.
This time, the geological formations were our
prominent focus. We took our time observing
the fascinating sandstone strata. We also went
slowly because we were both beat from three
solid days of hiking. Lisa was feeling it as
much as I. Truth is, I'm in considerable pain
as I write this but it was well worth it.

We hobbled back to camp, I put my bad leg
up for a while, had a snack, and took some
over-the-counter pain meds. This afternoon,
we'll finish getting ready to pull out. In the
morning, like Adam and Eve leaving paradise,
we will flee Zion.

And it's a good thing, too. The forecast
is calling for big rain. This campground can
flood. Once again, our timing proved excellent.
We had good weather when it counted and took
full advantage of the bad weather. We'll leave
before the thunderstorms.

Next, northwest Arizona and perhaps Vegas.

~ Rachel

Closing This Circle

From Zion, we headed to Las Vegas for a stay at the famous Red Rock Canyon but it was not to be. We boondocked one night just off the Vegas Beltway. The next morning, we arrived at Red Rock only to find the place closed.

Congress had shut the government down! WTF?

What do we do now?

We boondocked and planned a trip into northern California and the Redwood Forest, but that also didn't happen. Bad news from home came so we beat a retreat back east to Florida but we didn't get there either. We thought about where to stop on our way back to the Northeast. On the way back, we had a couple of good stops before turning off Interstate 10 to go north when things changed.

We very much loved the Shenandoah Valley and its Skyline Drive federal campsites on previous loops and we hoped to hit it again after Florida. Some camp spots along the Blue Ridge Parkway and Skyline Drive are primitive, and we used them on previous trips, but our favorite, Big Meadows, had a water hook-up, dump station, and paid showers. We aimed for that.

We loved Little Rock, Arkansas, with its reasonably-priced municipal campground right on the river with easy access into the city. In Arkansas, we also had previously stayed two weeks at a federal site in the Ozark National Forest but we didn't have time for that. We considered the Barber Motorcycle Museum in Alabama which I wanted to see again.

One stop that was often repeated on our way north or south was a place called Mayberry Campground, Near Mount Airy, North Carolina. That's where they filmed the *Andy Griffin* TV show! Nothing special about the place but this private park had discounts and was on route. I can't forget that tire repair shop near Mayberry. Our motorcycle trailer tires needed replacing. We got a tip and went to a local tire guy way out in the middle of nowhere. Parked outside were rare cars from the 1940s such as Tuckers and Nash cars, and one was an ambulance. I love that stuff. *Antiques Road Show* is my all-time favorite TV show. I showed such enthusiasm that the shop foreman called the owner to get permission to show me the "backroom". It was actually an attached warehouse stuffed with a collection to die for, including the best assortment of face jug pottery I've ever seen. I'd love to have stopped in there again.

On the way back we tossed around many ideas on where we could camp going back east after Florida. Where to stop along Interstate 10 heading east to Florida was the immediate question.

Lisa suggested, "How about the Mississippi Petrified Forest?"

You heard right, it's a real thing. Mississippi has a petrified forest. This privately owned campground wasn't bad, a nice little museum and interesting fossils but it was an in and out stop for us.

The family emergency morphed and forced us to change our plans again. We had to run for Florida quicker although we did get to see the Mississippi Petrified Forest beforehand. Alas, visiting many of our past favorite places on the way wasn't to be.

Almost there, we got word that our presence in Florida wasn't required so we decided to run back to Pennsylvania and so we hit the Blue Ridge and Mayberry once again. We ended the Big Loop where we started a year before.

On the road back to Pa. the old Dodge became extremely lethargic. The motor had been getting weaker over the years so we decided to rethink and make some changes before the next launch which is how we got into the Class-A.

Interesting to note we thought the Dodge was shot. We offered it for sale without much hope but we sold it for what we had paid for it although the motor was toast. The mechanic who bought it was very happy to have it.

Ruth Goldberg lives on!

SECTION THREE:

Tips, Tricks, Problems, and Solutions

I didn't know camping was so complicated.

In this section, we'll go over practical things we learned that you'll need to know. We'll talk about the typical problems and how to avoid or beat them. No doubt RVs have inherent problems and issues because of what they are. That is, many RVs have problems because of how they are made. They are built to save weight and to trick you into thinking RVs are just like home.

Remember, they aren't.

You should have some basic mechanical skills or a willingness to learn how to maintain your rig or the frugal motorhome gypsy life is not for you. At least, not full-time. And that is okay. Weekend campers will also benefit from our tips and tricks.

A Tale of Two Radiators: Learning the Hard Water Way

We thought we were ready. We studied the motorhome gypsy life and worked on perfecting the rig. But we missed the obvious and didn't know it until after we left our old life behind.

We already told you about our radiator disaster while heading south on our first loop. Going up and down the hills of Interstate 81 taxed the motor which told us the true condition of the cooling system. We had been forced to abandon the mountain highway in favor of flatter ground to ease the motor's struggle. That helped, but it wasn't enough.

We should have known something was up! There were clues. The previous owner had run three-inch PVC plumbing pipes under the grill and open to the front to ram in more air. I can't believe we missed that. We thought it was a backyard mechanic trying to improve ventilation as the air conditioning didn't work. We didn't suspect that the truck had an overheating problem. We found out the hard way, 500 miles from launch. As you saw, we boondocked in a truck stop which gave us time and space to deal with it.

We gave them truckers there quite a show — two old ladies taking the front of a Class-C apart surely had to be something they hadn't seen before. It would have been an even bigger issue if not for the fact I had worked in a radiator shop and knew how to solder radiators.

TIP: Carry tools when driving an old rig.

We had the necessary skills but didn't have soldering tools. One can't anticipate everything. Good thing we had our toad. That little motorcycle paid for itself that day. Lisa got the supplies and we patched the radiator together. It worked…for a while. After four months we limped back to Pennsylvania to attack and solve the problem.

One thing we did not do before leaving home was look inside the radiator. When we finally did thousands of miles later, we discovered the radiator choked with calcium. We continued the trip and nursed it along until it became critical. Bad idea. People need to know…

Never put anything but distilled water OR antifreeze in a vehicle's radiator.

I've always known that. Lisa taught it in shop class. The idea that somebody had put tap water (or worse yet, well water) into this cooling system never occurred to us. Oops.

TIP: Check the radiator before you buy a used rig. Make sure the cooling system and all other systems were cared for correctly.

A simple thing like water can ruin your radiator. I can't believe we got caught this way, twice. But you can't see the top of the radiator's core tubes with coolant present. You can remove the radiator cap when cold and stick a finger in there to feel around for lumps and scale deposits. I should have done that!

In the Class-C's case, the story ended well. We were able to buy a new-old-stock (NOS) copper radiator for two hundred bucks. What a bargain!

We solved that problem but the damages done to the motor were later realized. That radiator was so full of mineral deposits that when we cashed it in at a junkyard, we were paid twice the radiator's true weight value. Junkyards pay for scrap by weight and class of metal. That calcium weight translated into copper money. The scrap value of copper is high. We got 85 bucks out of that junk radiator, reducing our out-of-pocket cost for our NOS radiator to 115 bucks plus tax.

We did all the labor ourselves.

If you take a project like this to a shop, the expense will not be good. Almost anyone can unbolt a radiator and put it back in. This is why taking time to learn basic engine maintenance can benefit you. Ask the mechanically-inclined people you know or meet to help you. Get some extra tutoring on YouTube before taking to the road.

> **TIP:** If you need to replace a radiator, don't buy a factory replacement aluminum and plastic one. Plastic tanks break easily. Custom radiator shops can build anything you need if you can't get copper from the parts store. Well-built all-aluminum units work well, but that's custom stuff. Copper can be repaired; plastic and aluminum can't and copper is a better conductor of heat.

It's hard to believe we made this mistake twice and got stung by hard water again. Four years later, we purchased our 1990 Mallard Class-A rig. Guess what? When we looked at it, we didn't look inside the radiator. When we did, it was full of mineral deposits. Yikes!

Learn from our mistakes?!

> **TIP:** It's a good idea to drain the radiator once you own the truck to check for mineral deposits. Looking inside the radiator's cap won't tell the story unless it's empty.

The first thing I normally do with *any* new-to-me vehicle is check and change all of the fluids. Do that before shoving off.

How did we make this radiator mistake a second time? Bad assumptions. The owner had new exhaust manifolds put on and other work with all the receipts, so we assumed all was well. We should have checked. That new exhaust manifold was actually a huge clue. Why did the manifold warp?

Overheating, of course.

The rig was parked at the mechanic shop when we saw it. We picked the mechanic's brain, but we didn't pick deeply enough. On the way from Pennsylvania to my sister's house in New Jersey, the Mallard overheated. We employed our familiar drive slow technique and made it to my sister's house. (The refrigerator in that rig also died, but that's another story.)

Once we got the rig parked, we opened the radiator cap. This one was clogged worse than the Class-C! No wonder the seller had the exhaust manifolds replaced. The seller had driven it back and forth to hard-water

Alaska several times. That missed clue explained the heavy mineral deposits. There was more to learn, and this time we did a deep dive.

That radiator wasn't the only problem.

So, what did we do?

Lisa and I disassembled the entire front covering of the motorhome to get at the engine. We pulled everything off the front of the motor that could be replaced. We weren't messing around this time. We changed out all the belts, pulleys, hoses, alternator, and water pump. Whatever could be replaced was. We had to take the radiator out so why stop there?

This was smart of us. The cost savings on labor and replacing all these parts meant less problems later. We got ahead of issues before they were issues. If you had to pay somebody to do all that, it would cost several thousand dollars in labor plus parts. Ouch. Parts costs weren't bad for that big-ass gas motor.

What about the radiator?

How and where does one find a 1990 P30 truck radiator? The ones we did find were crap. Our solution: We hired a nearby custom radiator shop. They build radiators for hotrods and trucks. The original radiator was copper so we had the custom shop re-core it in copper and add a core with more rows of tubes. Radiator tubes run from the top tank to the bottom tank. The more core tubes you have, the cooler the motor will run and the more abuse it can take on steep inclines. Rebuilding the original was cheaper than starting from scratch. But this shop had the capacity to do either. We wanted the best we could get to reduce possible problems on the road.

> **TIP:** Hot rod shops are a good place to find creative solutions. A custom shop helped us later solve a crank sensor problem on that same rig.

We had more than one problem causing the overheating issue. The P-30 truck chassis supporting this Mallard motorhome needed air dams under the motor to direct hot air away from the engine compartment by way of the radiator fan. The motorhome builder of this rig had removed the air dam from under the passenger side to put their RV body on the truck's frame. Bad idea. This is why the former owner had to have the exhaust manifold replaced on one side repeatedly.

It wasn't all the radiator's fault. I made an air dam out of galvanized sheet metal and metal studs. Problem solved. She never ran hot again.

> **TIP:** If you buy a motorhome based on a truck frame, check under it to make sure it has airflow control dams. Dams are simply a few hunks of steel attached to the frame that direct air flow.

We had other issues with the Class-A Mallard that we didn't see until we were 130 miles from home, such as the two-way refrigerator died. Good thing we weren't gone for real yet! The buyer was kind enough to offer us $500 cash back. That was half the cost of a replacement at the time.

Before you take that long trip, drive an unfamiliar rig locally, not too far from home or whomever you bought it from. That work we did on the Mallard Class-A is not the kind of thing you can do in a truck stop parking lot.

Why RVs Suck

You have read some of the problems we encountered. These are common problems. You may think RVs have a lot of issues and you would be right.

| TIP: Active, handy people are best suited for RV living.

One of the issues of RV living is the human factor of managing your space. This is important because you don't have a lot of it. Your personality type must be considered. One can't be disorganized or lazy. The dishes can't wait because there is no room to pile them. A dirty rig invites insects and mice inside. Clean up or pay the price in discomfort. The waste tank can't wait either. Unless, of course, you enjoy the smell of poop.

RVs suck, in part, because you must keep after potential problems. RVs, be they self-powered or towed, are made light. That often equates to cheap or even shoddy construction. For example, a stainless-steel sink doesn't weigh more than a plastic sink, but many rigs provide nothing but plastic fixtures. A blazing hot pot or spilling frying oil in a plastic sink may well set the rig to flames.

I have seen it myself and heard many sad stories about badly-made RVs. They come out of the factory with issues. The manufacturer tells the dealer to fix it, but the dealers don't or they do a bad job. If you roll off the lot with a brand-new rig and find a problem, good luck getting the manufacturer or dealer to respond to your repair needs.

I know a snowbird couple who bought a new fifth-wheel of high quality from a star maker. This top-shelf rig sprung a leak in the roof within weeks. It took a year for the dealer to do something about it, and the buyer had to haul it from Florida to upstate New York to get the work done where it was purchased. In the meantime, that long wait propelled the owner to buy a huge, expensive garage structure to protect the leaky roof.

Another person I knew was more forceful and stopped payments on her new lot-home rig[16] and refused to pay until they fixed her issues. The local dealer went under, so with the threat of a lawsuit, this huge rig was shipped to the manufacturer. It took six months to get it back. Motorhome gypsies must plan for living arrangements during breakdowns. We need to rely on ourselves as you have seen but you can't always do that.

---

16   A lot-home rig is a travel trailer designed to sit long-term and not travel other than to and from long-term spots. Most are more than 30-feet long and can go to about 60 feet with more weight and more slide-outs than the typical camping rig. Most of them are too heavy to haul yourself. Lot-homes are delivered by the dealer or a professional house mover.

> **TIP:** If you buy from a dealer don't expect follow-up repair satisfaction.

Even if perfectly-made to the best of the builder's abilities, there will be problems. The nature of RV construction brings innate problems and some systems are naturally loaded with contradictions. They all have the same basic problems, but instead of finding new solutions, builders often copy each other's designs.

Dealers don't want to admit what they really know about how sucky RVs can be and that sucks. Sales people don't necessarily know the technical end and that sucks. Low-quality mechanics, I suspect, are not uncommon behind the shop doors. They will tell you, "Trust me, it's fine. Built to industry standards," but it ain't fine. "Industry standards" suck.

> **TIP:** Dealers want you to sign a sales contract, don't do that unless you understand it.

If you must have a contract for financing, have a lawyer look at it. Contracts aren't set in stone. One can add clauses or strike contract conditions. If they won't sell under your conditions, go somewhere else. If they want the sale, they will accept your conditions.

The typical sales contract generally indemnifies them from all responsibility, forcing you (as the buyer) to pursue the factory for warranty work. What if you live in Florida and the factory is in Illinois? Builders put money into selling and not development. They spend money on fancy decorations when practicality is better for long-term RVing. Industry standards are based on cost and the availability of materials and not on what best suits the buyer's needs.

> **TIP:** Look closely when you shop. Anything "house-like" is probably cheaply made.

Do not look at a rig, brand new or old, as a house or an equivalent replacement for normal living quarters. RV living is a different world. Sellers want you to believe it's just like home. Be practical first. Looks are superficial. "Homey" is a sales tool. Don't be fooled by pretty things.

> **TIP:** When shopping for a rig, consider how you will use it, what your practical needs are.

Do RVs suck? Yes, compared to a fixed home. But then again, try and haul your house 100 miles.

Reality Check: You will need to make repairs, and you will need to maintain the rig continuously yourself. RVs don't suck when you understand them and have learned how to work on them. The reason I'd rather buy a used rig, and why I would not buy from a dealer, is because at least some of the problems will have been addressed and other issues will be obvious. How else do RVs suck? Appliances. To be fair, there are pluses to the house systems that come with a rig. The systems and appliances are based on normal house stuff but they aren't the same as regular household appliances. These devices do the same jobs but are a lot smaller.

> **TIP:** Any appliance made for an RV will cost a lot more than an equivalent house unit.

RV appliances aren't really equivalent. The refrigerator, for example, may be the same overall size as an apartment unit, but the house unit will have a lot more interior space. A house size hot water heater won't fit in any RV. The stove is smaller. The list goes on.

One of the big downsides of RV interiors and mechanical systems is the use of plastic. In our 2000 Sunline travel trailer, the sinks, faucets, shower pan, shower walls, and faucet hardware are all cheap plastic. The 1978 Class-C was mostly built with regular home parts before RV-specific plastics became common. The 1990 Mallard, Class-A had a lot of plastic parts. Our 1999 Carriage fifth-wheel, a top brand of the day, had a combination of steel and plastic.

> **TIP:** Plastic fixtures don't last.

We changed out the RV-specific parts on all of our rigs wherever possible. When the plastic fails, (and it will!) upgrade. Stainless steel sinks weigh the same and cost less. Should you replace plastic parts with the same, you will pay a premium. RV parts are made cheaply but cost more than conventional. When replacing plumbing, appliances, or utility systems parts, upgrade to regular residential materials where possible.

> **TIP:** Never put a hot pan into a plastic sink. Plastic burns, and the fumes are toxic. Got a grease fire? The usual thing is to put the offending pan in the sink. Don't do that!

WARNING: Never use water to extinguish a grease fire! DO NOT put it in a plastic sink and run water. Cover the pan with a lid to smother the flames, or smother with baking soda, best yet is keep a fire extinguisher handy.

WARNING: RVs burn easily, toxicity, and quickly. Make sure your smoke detectors work! Never block your fire escape window. Make sure fire extinguishers are operable. Extinguishers do go bad.

Shower pans are a big issue. A shower pan is what you stand on while in the shower. Just like in a house, the pan can be part of a fiberglass shower enclosure, or the pan can be separate from the shower wall covering. Only larger and more expensive RVs will have one-piece shower stalls. The average RV will have the two-piece plastic setup. I've seen enough pans break to realize a systemic issue.

Plastic shower pans will crack. They are hard to replace. To replace a shower pan requires major surgery in most cases. On my Sunline, I had to take apart the inside walls and exterior siding to support the pan before repairs. Good thing my fifth-wheel came with a hard-core residential fiberglass shower stall because pulling that one out would be a nightmare. Big rigs and a few better-quality small rigs will have a one-piece, fiberglass shower. If you find one with such a design, put that rig at the top of your possible purchase list.

Plastic or fiberglass shower pans can be repaired in place with epoxy, plastic weld, and/or fiberglass and resin. In a pinch, for a crack or hole, you can use EPDM roofing seam tape (made from ethylene propylene diene monomer synthetic rubber) to keep the pan usable temporarily. Plumbing supply houses and some RV stores can order shower pans of almost any size. There are now manufacturers who make shower pans, bath enclosures, and sinks from Corian and other materials. These are much better than stock RV parts and can be shaped as you need.

> **TIP:** Before you buy any RV, check the shower pan. Get inside the shower and jump a bit. Hidden cracks will pop open. I've had to repair the shower pans in the Class-C, Class-A, and the Sunline. I repaired them in place.

Good news: Fiberglass repair is simple and less likely to be needed. Fiberglass is tough stuff. You can find YouTube videos to explain the basic process. With plastic pans, high-quality epoxies will hold them together unless the crack is traumatic. A badly broken pan usually means that it is not correctly supported underneath. The floor may have rotted from unseen leaks. If that is the case, the structural problem must be fixed first, which means, the pan must come out and be replaced.

> **TIP:** Keep a close eye on the shower pan in any RV. Depending on the issue, if you wait too long it can't be repaired in place. Carry a good quality epoxy on-board for repairs. (Use epoxy as directed.)

Why shower pans crack: How shower pans crack isn't usually to do with how they are made. Pans, home or RV, are designed to flex a little when stood on. When they move too much, they break. Pans are generally elevated off the floor deck to make room for drain and trap connections. For lift and support, pans have a foam block glued to their underside. Thus, the pan does not make direct contact with the floor surface. When this foam block deteriorates, or the floor under the block goes bad, the pan will flex beyond its safe range. Supporting the pan correctly prevents cracking and allows one to make a repair one can count on.

Sometimes, if you have access, you can shoot high density spray foam into the weak spot and support the pan. Before doing any patch repair it is imperative that you are certain the pan is properly supported otherwise it will crack again. If the floor under the pan block is shot, you have no choice but to rip it all apart and fix the floor issue. Plastic pans can age-out, i.e.: get brittle, and break even when properly supported. In that case it will have to be replaced. I've not seen a fiberglass pan age to that point.

The next item on an RV that sucks, try sleeping on a stock RV bed. That's one unpleasant wake-up call. RVs come with bad mattresses, unless you buy a very expensive bus with a real mattress. RVs usually come with memory foam mattresses. In our experience, memory foam sucks.

A mattress is an individual thing, and builders will provide the cheapest universal crap they can. Some of the fold-out sofas aren't bad for what they are, a guest bed, but sleeping on one every night sucks.

I don't know why builders feel compelled to include mattresses. Do you get a bed when you buy a house? You will probably wind up buying a new bed for your rig, and you can't pull any old mattress from your house. Many RV mattresses are odd-sized to fit odd spaces. There is no room for a box spring. RV mattresses bought at RV stores aren't any better than the one you want to replace. Have I mentioned that RV mattresses suck?

Don't rob yourself of a good night's sleep.

And if you're buying a used rig, new owners should trash that old, smelly bed anyhow.

| **TIP:** We use medical-grade air mattresses. They wear like iron and outlast any airbed you can buy off the camping store shelf. They are cheaper than regular house mattresses, and they can be ordered to fit any size. These air-fill hospital-grade units are washable and tough. We have had our queen-sized for more than eight years without a leak.

Airbeds weigh little whereas regular mattresses weigh a lot. We get beds for our rigs from New World Manufacturing, out of California. They build pool liners and medical-grade cushions of all kinds. We still have the two air mattresses that we bought for the Class-C years ago. We use them in the bug-out van now. The two we had custom-made for the Class-A went with the rig when we sold it.

What sucks, for new buyers, is going into a rig thinking it's a house and no different than house living. It is very different. Be aware. The quality of everything will suck. Every aspect is a compromise. If one isn't informed, that will suck. For instance, don't get rambunctious and slam the cabinet doors, they may well disassemble at the corners. The same goes for the drawers.

To add a few more things to the list...Towing sucks. Driving the big truck sucks. Trying to park all of that stuff sucks. Backing up sucks. But try not to get worried, one gets used to driving the rig. It is a learned skill. Driving the rig can become a mindful second nature habit with practice. But at first, it will suck.

Putting fuel in the rig or front-toad truck is gonna suck because any rig will be a monster gas-eater. The cost of driving sucks, but added up, it's still cheaper than rent.

Careful planning to save gas and resources may also suck, but Lisa and I enjoy the challenge. Consider figuring out how to maximize the impact of your funds as a game, and it's a little easier.

What may suck could be anything. It's different for each of us.

Going slow sucks if you like driving fast. You can't drive fast towing, that ain't safe. If you hate straightening up and organizing continually, you may have a bad time. If you love to let crap pile up until you are good and ready, you aren't going to have a good time living in a small box. If you hate doing systems maintenance, troubleshooting, and general upkeep to prevent real problems, you aren't going to relax and enjoy the motorhome gypsy life.

It may be that learning how to live the motorhome gypsy life, and all it entails, seems sucky to you.

But for us? We love this life and think it is worth it.

What doesn't suck — caring for the rig becomes a habit in time. We do the necessary stuff so we can do the fantastic stuff, such as hiking in Zion National Park or exploring the Army Corp of Engineers' Vally of Fire campground. RVing is the only way to reach fantastic places that you'll never experience otherwise. The great outdoors never sucks.

Okay, so maybe RVs don't suck. The tradeoffs are worth it...to us. We hope you'll think so, too.

The motorhome gypsy life is not static. It's full of activities. Yeah, some stuff will suck but, to us, life in a forest or desert feels a lot less sucky than rush-hour traffic.

RV Roofs

Up front, we told you about septic tanks because that is the number one problem unaware buyers have. Now, we'll tell you the other big problem RV owners always have, new or old.

If you had to guess, what would you say is the biggest issue with RVs? What is the one bug-a-boo every rig must struggle with?

Hint: It's a four-letter word — Roof.

I don't mean a barking dog: Roof, roof, roof! It's that thing above your head you never think about and the dealer didn't mention. Your RV roof will make you barking-dog mad. Here is a cold fact: RV roofs will leak. Expect it.

The ultimate roof system for rigs, which preceded modern production of motorhomes, was the best roof a travel trailer or motorhome can have: Aluminum. That's what you see on an Airstream or Argosy. You may have seen such a rig going down the road. These brands resemble a World War II aircraft fuselage on wheels. Airstream and Argosy wrap the entire body and roof in sheets of aluminum making them practically leak proof. Our Class-C had an aluminum roof. Aluminum roofs are tough and easy to fix.

Aluminum construction is not widely-used on RVs today. Aluminum-bodied brands are pricey, because the price of aluminum has increased. Shoppers will notice that new, used, and vintage Airstreams are expensive. Lots of people enjoy restoring, owning, and camping in vintage units. In my view, they aren't great to live in full-time, but they do tow nicely. The smaller Airstreams, in our opinion, are a great option for motorhome gypsies who want to travel often. A good choice, that is, if you have the money for one. Why so expensive? Aluminum!

Travel trailers and motorhomes from the 50s into the early 70s all had aluminum roofs. They only used a few sheets, if not one big sheet like on our 1978 Class-C. Fewer sheets means fewer seams, and fewer possible leak locations. Flat, rust-resistant metal roofs have no problem dealing with pooling water.

Old-fashioned metal roofs are simple to repair and maintain. Even a big hole can be fixed.

TIP: Epoxy is your friend.

This is how you fix a hole in a metal roof. Get another piece of sheet metal of the same type, make a piece big enough to cover and overlap the problem, lay down some epoxy, and pop-rivet the patch onto the surrounding roof. Both surfaces must be clean and dry. If the problem is where water pools, use a seam tape over the spot once the patch is riveted flat to a very well-prepared roof surface. Proper riveting alone can do the trick, but since you're up there anyway, go the extra mile.

Fiberglass was the miracle material of the late 1950s. That's when fiberglass boats came into prominence. You may have seen older RVs that look like an upside-down boat. I wondered why fiberglass isn't used more, and I learned the answer. It cost more. You won't see many fiberglass rigs on the road. One of the famous fiber-bodied rigs, revered and sought after by motorhome adventurers, is the Toyota, truck-based Class-C which we mentioned before. One of the best Toyota fiberglass brands is the Dolphin, but there are other brands on the Toyota frame also made with fiberglass bodies. Fiberglass is easy to fix and doesn't require special tools.

Fiberglass and metal roofs are rare today, mostly seen on older rigs or high-end rigs. This brings us to the most common RV roof these days — rubber. Synthetic rubber roofs are standard. Older RVs use a rubber roofing membrane called ethylene propylene diene terpolymer (EPDM). Newer rigs use thermoplastic polyolefin (TPO). Unless you buy a bus or fiber-bodied rig, you are getting a rubber-based roof. I use the word "rubber" loosely.

The first rubber-roofed rigs used commercial-grade, EPDM rubber sheet goods. EPDM and the subsequent similar products have continued to evolve. The first EPDM roofs were used on buildings. Thus, they were thick and durable. Later, the product was made thinner and cheaper for RV builders. Older EPDM products lasted between 15 and 20 years before they degenerated, but that is not why they leak. Transitions and penetrations are where and why they leak, even with a good roof in place.

In recent years, most RV manufacturers have switched to TPO roof material, still a rubber-like sheet. EPDM and TPO look the same and act the same, but you must know which one you have to care for it properly and to repair it correctly when it leaks. TPO is based on vinyl, and EPDM is based on synthetic rubber. Not every patch material will stick to both materials, be it caulk, liquid roofing, or seam tape. Let me repeat: *not all roofing repair products can stick to every roof.*

TIP: Always read the instructions! Never use roof tar! Never use silicone!

The material I used to recoat my Class-A roof is no longer available. That two-part epoxy was known as Liquid EPDM or Liquid Rubber. I bought the coating directly from the manufacturer of EPDM sheet goods. It welded to the existing EPDM like magic. You can't buy that stuff anymore. There are products on the market with the same name taking the place of two-part coatings, but I'm not convinced they work as well.

I knew EPDM and other sheet roofing products well when I ran construction jobs. My position required me to understand them fully. I also know that products change all the time, so every RV owner must do the research to understand the materials used in or on their rig. You must understand the materials and in what combination they will or will not work together before application.

I see this mistake all the time. People use the wrong products and get bad results. If you can't read the labels go to the manufacturer's website for application instructions and limitations. Don't trust random people on the Internet pontificating about products. Have doubts? Contact the manufacturer.

> **TIP:** If you know what you have and you know how to fix it you can assemble a repair kit to keep on the rig as you travel.

Why roofs leak has to do with sealing transitions between heights and or body parts and penetrations that go through the roof surface. Many leaks happen because of bad designs. Penetrations can't be helped. You need vent pipes, a refrigerator vent, and pretty much every RV air unit is mounted on the roof. Air unit mounting is not done well in my construction professional's view. They are mounted flat on the surface with a gasket, whereas curbing with curb-flashing and counter-flashed is way better. But that costs time and money. Guess what? Manufacturers don't like to spend!

On side body panels, at the roof's edge, the roof/body intersection typically has an aluminum gutter trim piece running front to back on both sides. Body panels — plastic, aluminum, or fiberglass — commonly use different materials than what is on the roof barring the high-cost exceptions. Wherever these two elements meet, roof to body, is a potential leak. Meeting dissimilar materials requires a special metal transition strip. That trim piece is installed by screwing it down with butyl tape under it to prevent screws from leaking. Screwing down a transition bar over two lapping materials is a bad weather sealing system. It's cheap, easy, and fast and that is why manufacturers do it.

How do you recondition that crappy bridging seam between body and roof?

Remove the metal trim, strip out the old butyl tape, install new butyl, and reassemble it. Then, you wait for it to leak again or...You can *really* fix it.

After stripping and rebuilding as above, use a self-sticking roof seam tape to completely bridge the repaired transition trim strip. Tape from the body panel to the roof surface. Go right over that nice, clean rebuilt metal transition trim strip. Bridge the two with that tape. Seam tape is flexible and will stretch. It also sticks on any clean surface as if welding steel-to-steel. It has a smooth top surface. If it rips, you can clean it off and add a new piece. Lap and layer it any way you like. This stuff can take the place of caulk or flashing if used well and with care.

> **TIP:** Never go anywhere without seam tape. My Sunline roof is covered in it.

I love the seam tape product called Eternabond. It's used in commercial roofing (more knowledge from my time in construction). Good stuff, but it ain't cheap. Then again, it's cheaper than a ruined floor. It comes in various sizes. I like the 4-inch and 6-inch-wide rolls. This stuff is pretty bulletproof. Because of how sticky it is, it is hard to use. I recommend working with short lengths and lapping them for ease of installation.

> **TIP:** Seam tape is stickier when warm than when cool. You can use temperature as a tool (hair dryer or refrigerator) to suit your needs.

RVs also have body seams with trim strips, similar to roof transition strips, on vertical corners. There are a variety of styles but all are installed over the body panel with butyl tape behind it like the roof transition strip. These body trim parts need occasional rebuilding. The rubber gasket covering it may turn ugly, but what's behind that cover, which you can't see, is what matters. Screws holding down that trim do rust out. This allows water to penetrate the body. Keep an eye on your body trim.

> **TIP:** Every five to ten years, depending on conditions, remove body trim and repack it with butyl before it leaks.

IMPORTANT: Not all RV roofs are safe to walk on. The easiest way to tell if your roof is a walk-safe roof is the presence of a ladder — rigs with ladders mounted at the rear usually have walkable roofs. If your travel trailer, like my Sunline, doesn't have a ladder attached to the body, don't go up there. If you need to make repairs on a non-walkable roof, buy some plywood and cut it to fit between penetrations. Use this plywood to bridge between rafters so you don't suddenly wind up inside the rig. But don't walk on the plywood either, scoot along on your butt!

Our 1978 Class-C had rotting plywood under the siding at the exterior corners. The body's construction was framed with two-by-two wood wall studs, plywood sheathing over that, and horizontal aluminum siding installed, similar to house siding. This rig did not have one-piece body panels as is common now. The corners leaked water and rotted the plywood, which, in turn, rotted some of the wood framing. It looked fine from the outside.

TIP: To know if the plywood is rotten, push on the body with your hands. If wet, it will feel spongy. If dry-rotted, you'll hear and feel bits of wood crumbling.

TIP: To reinforce corners, use a metal wall-stud framing part known as a "90," which is a 2x2 inch galvanized piece of lightweight metal bent longways into a right angle. These typically come in ten-foot-long pieces. This material is very handy for reinforcing weak corners. Slipping a 90 in behind your siding at the corner is not hard to do. One can pop-rivet it to the siding as needed. Light gauge metal stud framing materials are useful for lots of repairs. C-channel-shaped metal studs and 90s can be purchased at lumber yards and home improvement box stores.

TIP: Add a pair of tin snips and a pop-rivet gun to your tool kit.

Which roofs are the best? I like solid aluminum. Fiberglass is close behind, although fiberglass-bodied rigs have their problems. I'm not a fan of working with fiberglass, either, but it's not hard. EPDM or TPO is what you are likely to be stuck with, so be ready to deal with it.

Should you spend a God-awful amount of money to buy a rig with the ideal roof?

Sure, if you have money. Most motorhome gypsies aren't rich. We do things on the cheap because we must, but we can't cheap-out on roof upkeep. Lisa and I do things ourselves because it's necessary, and it's cheaper. Doing it *well* is worth the time and money because it saves money and headaches in the long run. Plus, you know it was done right.

How many times can you patch a roof? Once, if you do it right.

Recoating RV Roofs

You can recoat your EPDM or TPO roof with products designed to do so. Be dang sure you know what's on your roof before you buy coating material. Not all compounds will stick. Again, doing a recoat yourself is simple and fun, but doing it wrong will suck. If you can roll out paint, you can recoat your roof.

Better roof systems *are* needed. RV builders aren't going to do that, unless, of course, it's on the high-money end of the RV spectrum.

RV roofing professionals and their magic products are on the march. These systems remind me of construction scams, because some of them are. Good luck finding somebody that will recoat your roof the traditional way and do it well. Some of these new products I accept as viable. None of them have been around long enough to make good on the lifetime warranties they claim to offer. These super roof recoating systems come under all sorts of fun marketing names: Lifetime Roof, Amour Roof, Iron Roof, Steel Roof, Roof Roof Arf, you get the picture. You must carefully examine their materials, and their claims about it, and *check references* before you hire one of these services when you can't do the job yourself. Super roofs, and I use the term ironically, come in several configurations. You can't buy super-roof products, they are proprietary. The product comes and leaves with the installers.

For recoating it yourself, or to supply a hired handyman, there are two-part epoxy-type roof coating materials and single-part coatings, both spirit-based on the market. The other common roof coating products are water-based acrylic. Spirit-based products are hard to clean and require chemical cleaners like mineral spirits or acetone. Similar coatings are supplied by proprietary contractors but these have special formulas infused with plastic or Kevlar. Such coating products, off-the-shelf or proprietary, are applied on top of the existing surface.

Don't forget aluminum, TPO, and EPDM require different coating materials. Not all recoating products will stick to one or the other. Be sure of what you have and if whatever miracle product you are considering will stick to it.

|TIP: *Nothing* sticks to silicone.

I recently researched the devil out of these products. I almost hired one of the big RV roofers. They are a prominent company in my area but they didn't pass my sniff test. I asked a lot of technical questions. The product I looked into won't stick to EPDM without extra primer stages, and extra stages mean more money. Even after adding whatever additional coatings are necessary to use their special top coat, that product, to me, was not ideal. Mr. Sales Guy put me on the phone with a technician, and our discussion confirmed this product wasn't for me. Mr. Sales Guy didn't know that. We dodged a bullet by digging for the deeper story.

I believe in the *concept* of a permanent, never-going-to-leak RV roof, but I know there is no such thing. If these new roof products work long-term — and on paper some look like they will — it's the best thing you can do for yourself. Coat it and forget it. No more caulking or leaks. What a dream!

We had our Carriage fifth-wheel roof done with a Kevlar-infused acrylic. I'm getting too old to climb and work on roofs. Frankly, if I still had my equipment and access to a good sheet metal provider, I would do my roof in metal. Aluminum is the only real RV super roof.

How does one recoat an RV roof with a coating product?

It's the same simple process no matter what recoating materials are used. Clean the existing roof completely, remove old caulk, and recoat according to the product's directions and reapply the correct caulk once the new coating has healed.

Caulk, Caulking & the Roof

People seldom maintain their roofs correctly. The biggest issue we have seen is people using the wrong caulk.

Never use silicone caulk, ever.

TPO and EPDM like the same kinds of caulks: rubber-based, urethane-based, butyl rubber-based, Lexan, and acrylic. Read the labels and follow the manufacturer's suggestions!

Never caulk over dirt or grease.

Every RV store sells a certain butyl-based caulk. I won't mention the brand name. It works okay for a few years. Most new rigs have this stuff blooped thick onto every transition. The problem is that it shrinks over time and opens, which allows water in. Most RV shops and rig owners will simply glob more of this same material on top of the old.

Never do that. Such an application won't cure the leak, but it will successfully hide it, short-term.

TIP: Always remove the old caulk and clean well before applying new material.

Improper caulking is a huge problem. There are two prongs to improper caulking. Wrong material is one issue. The other is poor application.

Every time you need to re-caulk, do it right or suffer the consequences. Clean the area to be caulked. And then clean it again. I hit it with acetone or alcohol after a couple of good washes with degreasing soap, with thorough rinses between each wash. The surface must be dry before you continue with the process.

And just to be sure you heard me, repeat after me: *Never caulk over old caulk!*

As for installation, keep in mind that more is not better. Just the right amount is best. Too little can be touched up later. You want a smooth, consistent bead, less than one-half inch wide for most applications. I cut my caulking tubes at the one-quarter inch mark. If you want more info, talk to a professional painter or carpenter. Better yet, let him (or her) show you. Applying caulk well takes a certain touch — and you can learn it.

Fixing leaks with caulk may not work. But the right caulk for the job will hold. The wrong caulk won't stick for long. The wrong caulk will leave a residue that the correct material won't like.

What's better than caulk?

That depends.

When it comes to transitioning from one surface to another, as I said before, you can't beat seam tape. That seam where the body meets the roof in the front and back of practically every rig is a troublemaker that caulk can't fix. Caulking there creates a mess and won't last.

Nothing is better than caulk when used correctly *for the right purpose.*

Dump pumping

Waste tanks are an uncomplicated utility. The only moving parts are dump valves. Those valves do need to be replaced from time to time, a simple job anyone can do. Normal dumping is done by way of gravity. Hook your sewer pipe to the inlet provided, pull the dump-valves open, and the tank's contents rush out. Close the valves and you are done.

TIP: We dump the black first so the gray can afterwards flush out the hose.

What if you need to push chunky tank waste uphill?

There's a utility device used to facilitate dumping waste tanks called the macerator pump. That's a powered gizmo that hooks onto the dump valve outlet of an RV. The macerator grinds anything solid into juice and pushes that waste through a garden hose. Some newer rigs have this built-in. Lisa and I do not like them built-in; it strikes us as one more built-in complication. Portables are better in our view. They are rarely necessary but small and easy to store if you have a need.

Why would you need a macerator pump?

Normally, you won't.

If you don't have access to a regular RV dump station, you can pump your waste into any toilet or a residential clean-out access point, such as a house trap. If you don't poop in your tanks, and remember, if you can avoid it, you should not poop in your tanks, any twelve-volt utility pump, such as a trash pump, AKA, impeller pump, that accepts garden hoses will work to pump liquids. The trash pump works by impeller blades such as a swimming pool or a fish tank pump. One can find these utility pumps cheap at Harbor Freight, Tractor Supply and hardware stores.

TIP: Never put solids through an impeller pump. Use a macerator type.

Let's look at this more closely.

When we park at my sister's house, for example, we stay in the rig and plug into the house's 110-volt electrical service. We aren't getting up at 3 a.m. to pee in her house. We use the black tank. We don't need an off-site dump station to empty the tank while there because we don't poop in it or put paper in.

Our cheap, twelve-volt impeller pump is all that's required. Via a garden hose used only for black water, we push the *liquid-only* contents 100 feet out, eight feet up the wall, through my sister's bathroom window, and into her toilet. That Harbor Freight pump cost $15 bucks when we got it years ago. All you need is enough garden hose to reach the target. Our cheap-ass pump will push wastewater 200 feet outbound and ten feet uphill.

We carry three different garden type hoses: One for potable water (made special for drinking water), one for utility use, and one for wastewater only.

When we stay at our friend's farm, we pump our tanks into their septic system, 150 feet across flat ground. No problem.

TIP: This kind of garden hose-adapted pump is cheap because it's not RV-specific.

Macerators are RV-specific and cost a ton. The only time you'll need a macerator pump is if you have no other way, like if you have a tiny inlet for dumping and a black tank full of trouble.

But keep in mind, macerators will not make your clogged tank any less clogged.

Having a portable twelve-volt macerator, or impeller pump, with you on the road is advisable. We used our impeller pump more than we expected.

TIP: If you must use a pump and must poop in the tank, get the macerator. That works best with single-ply toilet paper. Save the fancy multi-ply stuff for gas station poops.

One more time, let me say — we don't put paper in the black tank. Nothing but liquids, please.

TIP: Get a "poop bag." What's that? We carry it for poop stops on the road. It's a basic shoulder bag holding toilet paper, hand cleaner, soap, paper towels, wet-wipes, and alcohol wipes for cleaning the seat. It makes any nasty gas station bathroom viable.

One more note on tanks. Our new neighbor came for the winter in his brand new 30' travel trailer. Week three he had a flood inside. He'd forgotten the gray tank was closed and had left water running in a sink. When the gray tank filled, it backed up into the shower (the lowest place inside the rig) which proceeded to overflow the shower pan and soak his floor before he caught on. Fortunately, it was only the gray tank and so not too stinky.

Pay attention to your tanks. Keep an eye on the tank level indicators, if they work, but don't trust them. Level indicators are usually inaccurate.

Potable Water Tanks

RV's on-board fresh water (potable water) supply tank will hold anywhere from 25 to 75 gallons or more of cool, clear, clean freshwater. Your rig's paperwork will tell you capacity. While on the road, boondocking, or parked where there is no city water, you can still cook, clean, bathe, drink, and flush with the water you have on-board.

But WAIT!

Is that water pure, fresh, and clean?

How long has that water tank sat empty?

How old is that water anyway?

This may not be important for flushing, but for cooking and especially drinking, you want pure water.

Once or twice a year, depending on usage, your water system needs to be sanitized. Flushing is easily accomplished using a bit of household bleach and water mixture together. (Use one ounce of bleach for every eight gallons of freshwater of tank capacity). Allow this mixture to sit in the tank overnight and then flush it through the system to sanitize the pipes as well.

After a thorough rinse or two, you are ready to refill with clean fresh water. Always use a potable water hose to refill or hook up. Potable hoses are usually white or sky blue. Never use the potable hose for anything except potable water and cap the ends, or hook them together when not in use.

We have found it beneficial to filter our water. We used a number of water supply sources in our travels, and one never can be sure if the water is pure. With city water, it is best to filter water going into the holding tank with a sediment filter only. Chlorinated city water makes water lines and the tank cleaner. We use a sophisticated, carbon-block filter at the kitchen sink for drinking and cooking water, not caring for the taste of chlorinated water.

City water should be cleaner than well water but don't depend on the city or campground to provide clean water. Wherever we hook the camper to an outside water source we filter it. We carry two types of whole house water filters with us, one for chemicals and the other for sediments. No unfiltered water enters our rig.

Most RV parks, be they state, federal, or private, do have good water. Hard water and its mineral sediments are healthy to consume but also a problem. Hard water may be good for your bones, but not so good for your rig's pipes, faucets, and truck's radiator. We strongly suggest you carry a whole-house type water filter with you. We store and transport our portable house filters and potable hose, capped off and sealed, inside the rig's shower stall as we drive.

Getting Jacked and Level

Once we had a loose wheel on the Class-C, and it took two jacks to lift the truck enough to tighten the lugs. *Be sure to have a jack rated for your rig*, a big-ass breaker bar, jackstands, and a hardcore lug wrench.

You shouldn't — and wouldn't — change a flat on a big rig yourself, but you may need the tools anyway. If you get stuck in the sand or mud tire-changing jacks might save your skin.

Newer Class-A and C rigs usually have powered leveling-jacks built-on. Push a button and they extend. These are intended to stabilize a parked rig. I can't tell you how many rigs I've seen where they forgot to raise the stabilizer jacks before pulling out. This, of course, destroyed them.

Leveling-jacks of any kind are not designed to raise a rig high enough to change a tire.

Older motor rigs don't usually have powered leveling-jacks, nor do travel trailers in general. Towable rigs have manual stabilizer jacks at the corners which can't lift the rig's weight either.

To level our rig on a campsite we use pressure-treated two-by-eight wood planks. We roll the rig onto them as necessary. We can layer our planks three or even four high. We back-cut the ends of the planks at 45–degree angle so tires can roll on easier. Each plank is a little shorter than the next. Before pulling into a site, we run a level across the ground (side

to side) from one proposed tire spot to the other before parking. If the rig is level from side to side at the wheels, the rest is easy. Minor front to back leveling is what the built-in stabilizers are for.

> **TIP:** Be sure to carry a two or four-foot level. One can use a plank with the level on top to extend reach.

We also carry blocks to use under the stabilizer jacks. These are cut-off pieces of four-by-four pressure treated lumber. We also make chocks out of the same material. Never toss leftover wood!

A Practical Warning About Leveling: You will encounter unlevel sites. It is important to level the rig as close to flat as possible because a refrigerator running on LP gas can burn out the boiler tank!

When not level, the fluid in the boiler goes to one side, leaving the flame to build too much heat on the metal. The fluid inside disperses heat. A level camper is a happy camper. It also makes sleeping, cooking and eating more pleasant.

RV two-and three-way refrigerators use ammonia as a cooling fluid instead of freon. Ammonia contained inside a closed pipe loop under heat and pressure has a thermal reaction which generates cooling ammonia gas. That gas circulates through cooling coils. When on electric, the 110-volt heater does that job. The two-way feature burns LP gas for heat when off shore power. In a three-way unit, there is also a 12-volt heating coil. How burning gas keeps a refrigerator cold is scientifically complicated and we won't get into the details here.

> **TIP:** If you smell ammonia, your refrigerator is trash. Leaking RV refrigerators cannot be repaired. Avoid breathing the vapors and ventilate the rig. Toss the food.

RV Floors

Chances are the floor in your used rig needs attention. If it's got carpeting, get rid of it. RV carpeting is builder-grade cheap crap. Old carpeting is dirty, hard to clean, ugly, and holds odors you didn't make.

If you want to add floor ceramics, first use a cement board subfloor and employ mosaic tiles. Any large tile, even a four-inch square, will crack. Why? Primarily because everything *moves* when the rig is in motion. You might think you can avoid that issue by parking permanently, but even then, problems arise from the natural expansion and contraction of building materials caused by temperature and humidity flux. Larger tiles will crack.

Tongue-and-groove slat vinyl, like Pergo, is popular. These slat materials are cheap. You can do it yourself with a few tools. Such materials give you a decent life span. I used tongue-and-groove, ⅜ inch bamboo in our Class-A. Bamboo is light, looks great, and practically indestructible. You can't go wrong with hardwoods.

> **TIP:** Go to any floor supplier and ask them if they have leftovers from a job. This can get you steep discounts on quality material. Rigs don't have a lot of floor space. What's left from a house remodel is probably more than enough for your rig.

This trick works for more than just floors. Building suppliers often have leftovers, overstocks, and damaged or discontinued materials. I bought the cabinets for the Class-A remodel out of the damaged goods aisle. My bamboo floor was a supply house leftover.

Floor Maintenance: A small but powerful shop vacuum covers most of your motorhome needs. You can suck water or dirt. Just be sure to read the instructions before you vacuum water. You won't need a big-ass mop and pail. A large car wash sponge will do the trick. You will want a broom and dustpan.

Internet ready

Even if you want to escape the grind and you dream of off-grid living, like most people, you will need an Internet connection. If not used for entertainment, there is communications, banking, and shopping. The Internet sure is handy for mapping routes and making reservations. Good news!

Most commercial campgrounds provide wi-fi as do some stores. Be prepared to deal with an inadequate signal from your campsite.

Boondockers might have a phone for an Internet connection, but don't count on reliability. Good reception is hard to find in some places. Unfortunately, when we were on the Big Loop, our cell phone plans prohibited tethering for mobile data. Today, phone plans offer a lot more flexibility so depending on your plan and the geographic reach of your carrier that may be less of an issue. So, how do you deal with crappy wi-fi reception?

|TIP: Get a long-range wi-fi receiver/booster, known as a parabolic antenna. Ours resembles a tiny satellite dish and plugs into a USB port on our laptops. Roof-mount types are available for RVs. These have a greater range than portable units. Fixed units cost more, and if you mount one on the roof, it is a leak waiting to happen.

Our dish picks up wi-fi signals a city block away. While boondocking in parking lots, we connected to open wi-fi networks at neighboring stores. These dishes also make it easier to create a stable connection on a campground's wi-fi when your site is too far from the source.

Bathing & Washing

This section includes our tips for your RV bathroom, primarily regarding plumbing, functionality and everyday life.

Shower doors: Once they break, get rid of them. Some rigs come with accordion-type shower doors. They always break. We suggest a simple shower curtain and expansion rod.

Why?

The cheap shower curtain will give more room inside the tiny shower stall.

TIP: Use a curved shower rod for more room. If you can't get a curved rod, make one out of galvanized fencing top rail. Rent or borrow an EMT conduit pipe bender and shape it to your liking.

PRO TIP: If you go with a shower curtain, get the hooks that are made to hang two curtains, one inside and one outside, but only use one side of the double hook.

Why?

The not-used side is great for hanging drip-drying articles like soap-on-a-rope, wash scrubby, and swimsuits. Ladies, need I mention your unmentionables?

TIP: Wash basins are your friend. Plan on washing the dishes and your unmentionables outside. You don't have a lot of room inside, right? Cheap plastic wash basins are good for a lot of things — and if you decide to cook a mess of fresh mudbugs, remember that shellfish tastes better without mud so fill that tub, put your live crayfish in, and give them a nice bath. Wash-basins are handy for washing anything outside.

Plumbing fixture: I've said it before but I'll say it again: Avoid replacing RV sinks, shower diverters, and faucets with RV-specific items. They always cost more and are cheaply made. Use household materials whenever and wherever possible.

Tools & Handy Items

- **Basic items to carry on board:**
  Epoxy.
- Roofing seam seal tape.
- Mechanical and home repair tools, spare fuses and bulbs, a screw gun.
- Bow saw or chainsaw, ax, and a hatchet to cut firewood.
- Whatever tools are required to work on gas and hose fittings.
  Spare parts, especially sewer hose parts.

Garden Tools

What the hell am I talking about? Didn't you become a motorhome gypsy to escape mowing the lawn? Think carefully about this. You will be in the woods, and sometimes you'll need to clear some space and cut firewood. For safety, tools should be kept in the basements.

- Here's our woodsy list:
- One hand-held old-fashioned weed scythe. You swing it like a golf club. It's light and fits inside basement storage compartments.
- Bow saw.
- Ax.
- Hand hatchet.
- Small spade shovel (I also use it for metal detecting.)
- A collapsible leaf rake.
- Hot glue gun.
- If you have room, a chainsaw is handy, but you aren't likely to use it much. Manual ring-handle chainsaws are pretty effective in a pinch.

Other Must Have On-board Tools

- Safety jack stands.
- Big wrenches to work on hitches, wheel fittings, gas fittings, and stuck sewer screw caps.
- A breaker bar with whatever sockets fit your big nuts is imperative.
  A big-ass jack rated for lifting the rig or truck.

Dehumidifiers and Fans: Mold is a huge problem in wet states like Georgia and Florida. We use dehumidifiers in the house rig and in the storage trailer during the wet season. Exhaust fans help keep the humidity down when showering but not a perfect cure. Keep a close eye on humidity. We hang a simple humidity monitor on the wall. On the flip side, if you winter or summer where it's dry, use a humidifier for comfort. There are very small and effective units of humidifiers and dehumidifiers on the market.

Sewer hose spreader: A hose spreader works like an old-time shoe stretcher.

Why do you want this?

Try attaching an end piece onto a corrugated RV sewer hose without this tool.

Suitcase Solar Panels: As the name declares, these are small, portable, and will charge your house batteries. These are indisputably necessary for long-term boondocking. They don't take up much room. We had a crappy-by-today's-standards, 45-watt unit in our early motorhome gypsy days. In our Class-C, we routinely boondocked for two weeks or more without a generator or plug-ins. We lived very well on the house battery, hand-pumped water, and outhouses. We also could go two weeks on our on-board water (which uses a twelve-volt pump). Electricity never ran dry. The portable solar panel makes longer boondocking possible.

Bugs and critters: Once using the park's bathroom I opened the door and a small venomous snake fell off the top of the door. *Check before you enter any campground facility.* You might, and probably will, find spiders, snakes, frogs and or rats enjoying the facilities. We have seen bears and even a panther in unexpected places.

Don't forget a wasp and hornet spray. Also — have a book or computer resource on hand that shows you what's dangerous and what's edible where you camp. Don't go into the forest blind. We have a copy of the U.S. military survival guide. Get familiar with the local wildlife wherever you go to avoid problems.

Water pressure reducers: This is another off-the-shelf item you need. Why?

Because some parks have excessive water pressure and that can cause leaks and breaks in your plumbing systems. Screw the pressure reducer onto the camp's water supply spigot and hook your hose to that. Don't forget to take it when you decamp. I got a box full of left-behinds.

Electrical reducers: These are plug adapters so you can use your house connection on any power supply. What if you pull into a 50-amp hook-up site and have a 30-amp service plug? Use the adapter. You still get 30 amps without taking the full 50. It works in the other direction, too. If you have a 50-amp plug and only a 30-amp hook-up is available, same deal. Adapters come in all configurations. They are made to adapt to other types of outlets you may encounter (but they do not change the power available). On the last Sunline trip, we only had a 20-amp hook up at landing. With an adapter, we were able to use our 30-amp plug to pipe 120V into the rig. It was enough to run the lights, refrigerator, charge the batteries, and run the air (as long as nothing else was running).

Extension cords: You got an electric chainsaw? Like to play the radio outside? You will need a regular 110V extension cord. We also keep a 30-amp extension cord on the rig in case shore power is a longer distance than the rig's umbilical. They are rarely necessary, but handy if needed. Such heavy wire cords aren't cheap. We got ours at an RV dealer's fire sale for pennies on the dollar. It's not hard to make a cord, but if you aren't skilled in electrical work, forget making your own.

Pedal bikes: Bicycles are easy to bring along and very handy around camp. We have baskets on ours which we use to collect firewood. Bikes are easy to carry. Bike racks are cheap and can be mounted front or rear. RVs with ladders make it easy. RV stores sell a bike rack designed to mount on the rig's ladder.

Buddy heaters: Buddy Heaters are small propane heaters that run off a one-pound bottle. Buddy Heater is also the brand name.

Why do you need that? You may not, but here are a couple of reasons.

First, what if you are boondocking and get caught without battery power? Your on-board furnace needs twelve volts to run the controller and fan. Second, we used it a lot in campground bathhouses that were without heat. We also pack a small electric heater for when hooked up.

Note: You can hook a 20-pound tank to the Buddy Heater, but you will need a special hose and a filter made for that. Have I mentioned that one pound LP tanks are crazy expensive?

RV WARNINGS

Do not block or disable your emergency escape window.

RVs all have escape hatches because RVs burn fast and toxic. If you need a window air conditioning unit to replace a faulty roof air, do not put it in your escape window. We often see this. If you must use or block that window, add another escape window somewhere else. RV windows aren't hard to install. We added one in the fifth-wheel behind the bed's headboard. That's an ideal spot.

> **TIP:** No room for window air? Don't want another highly expensive roof air unit? Look into air units called mini-splits.

Body maintenance

RVs leak; of that you can be sure. Roofs are the usual suspects, but the body can leak, too. Check your corners and windows for tight seals *before you buy*. Inspecting body penetrations will often head off leaks. It is wise to address body and roof issues before they become a hidden leak. Body parts can let in water for years before you have a clue.

> **TIP:** Visually inspect your rig's overall condition often. Look for bad seals and open caulk seams.

If you are gonna fix up an old rig yourself, get one with horizontal aluminum siding. You can remove the siding, fix water damage, and put it back together with ease. Laminate body panel rigs look like a patchwork quilt after body parts are removed and reinstalled.

Fire Extinguishers and Detectors:

It is beyond important that you check the condition of your fire extinguishers. Rigs usually come with one but they are date sensitive and do go bad. Keep two with the rig, one for inside and one for outside, and keep one in the truck you tow with. If you don't have smoke, carbon dioxide and propane detectors, get them, do it now! Check the batteries often.

Non-Walk Roofs

Not all rigs have roofs capable of holding a person's weight. *This is important.* If the rig doesn't have a ladder built-on, chances are good that the roof *cannot* be walked on.

About RV Stores

I won't name the chains, but RV store clubs are not a bargain. Whatever you can buy online or used, do that first. We have seen firsthand how RV stores and dealers jack up prices, even sometimes, when they have a sale!

We have seen "on sale" items way cheaper elsewhere even with the club discount! We use RV stores for what we can't find any other way. Don't get us wrong, we love a good RV store! They have things and ideas you'll need and lots of fancy doo-dads that look alluring but you can easily do without. But be careful! Check your prices at alternate sources before you buy!

Eating on the Road

With the motorhome gypsy lifestyle, everything related to food will change. Maybe you're used to fast food. Maybe you like premade foods you simply heat. In your former life, maybe you were too busy to cook. In our modern fast-paced society, food is something you do to survive and move on to the next thing, whether it's your favorite television show or getting the kids to bed.

In the RV life, food preparation and consumption are features of daily life that you will not get through quickly. And you shouldn't use the RV life to eat all your favorite junk food. Lisa and I lost 30 pounds during our time on the road because we ate better.

Let's look at the reasons *why* we ate better.

First: Storage. Bags of chips and sugar-infused cereals take up a lot of valuable room. If it doesn't have nutritional value, why waste precious space?

Second: Cost. If you were attracted to the motorhome gypsy lifestyle to save money, remember that fancy junk snacks and processed foods cost a lot for no benefit. No bang for your bucks.

Third: Energy. You need real calories and not sugar rushes. If you got into the motorhome gypsy lifestyle to experience more, travel and do things, you will need nutrients to enjoy the great outdoors. Good food improves stamina.

When money is tight or stress is high, people gravitate to comfort food. Don't do that! Healthy food will save you money, maintain your health, and allow you to live life to the fullest. Healthy food is cheaper because it takes less of it to satisfy your body's needs. Junk food leaves you wanting so you stuff yourself with more resulting in nothing good.

If you never cooked or only know the basics, this lifestyle will allow you to learn camp-cooking. I hope you will adapt, and if so, we are sure you will enjoy it. The process of cooking is one of the joys of living close to the earth. Basic foods of good quality become the default because it's practical, cheap, and makes sense for travel and camping. In the wild, you'll have time to cook and time to think about what you are cooking. A few simple, quality ingredients can make a fantastic meal. Consider what will store well in limited space. The motorhome gypsy life demands it.

You won't find a fast-food joint in the middle of a national reserve. At times, we drove more than 100 miles without seeing *any* chain food whatsoever.

Don't get us wrong — you aren't going to stop eating out. In between camp stops, you will discover eats that are healthy, cheap, and unexpected. We learned to love truck stop BBQ but there is more. We once stopped at a gas station in Alabama, in the middle of nowhere, of course, and had homemade Boudin which is a Cajun-seasoned sausage of pork and rice. I never heard of it before, and it's yummy. Rice and pork, how can you go wrong? At another gas station stop off Interstate 10 I bought the best BBQ turkey leg I ever had.

One of my favorite roadside stops was at a taco truck in a Mexican-American family's yard near Stockton, Texas. It was the best Mexican food truck taco I ever tasted. The locals who passed by didn't share our enthusiasm. We saw more than our fair share of stink-eyed white guys in pickup trucks driving past. We ate there anyway and often. We loved that food. And, besides healthy, it was cheap!

TIP: Look for local foods by local people. Ask around.

Roadside ma-and-pa eateries are usually healthier, cheaper, and tastier than what chains offer. We always go where local people eat first. We seek out old diners and food trucks. Part of exploring the nation is exploring the food and trying new things. We especially go for BBQ. We made BBQ part of our travel priorities. Ironically, the best ribs I've had so far were in Pennsylvania. Ribs aren't a habit of ours. You can find the best BBQ, fried chicken, and seafood for less money and far better quality than any chain can offer if you take the time to look. That goes double for seafood. Want a fish sandwich, why not get it fresh?

In Aransas Pass, Texas, we learned about what is called a southern seafood boil. We found a fish shack on the docks where the fishing boats offload their catch. Never can you find fresher seafood than to go down to the docks, which I had learned as a child living at the New Jersey shore. Dock sniffing works wherever fishing takes place.

What blew us away, besides being cheap, was how good it was. Oysters normally ain't cheap. You only order a few because of the cost, if you can find them. Not so in that Texas fish shack. We didn't hesitate to order a dozen oysters each — fresh out of the Gulf! How can you beat it? Let's see — eat a dozen oysters with free bread and homemade horseradish red sauce for ten bucks or get the Big Mac three towns over?

Seems like a no-brainer.

TIP: When near a coast, find the fishing fleet.

If you go to Boston, go where the lobstermen dock in Scituate. In New Jersey, find the party boats dock in Point Pleasant. You can find and visit the fish markets and docks everywhere from California to Michigan — because yes, the Great Lakes count! If you like seafood and want it cheap and fresh, that's how you get it.

You can find good eats anywhere. Little Rock, Arkansas, has a massive foodie area right on the city's riverfront with lots of vendors cooking exotic fare. This is where I first tried mudbugs, commonly known as crayfish, crawfish, or crawdaddies. Can't get those in Pennsylvania! We also had Vietnamese food for the first time, and we loved it.

Cooking on the Road

How to cook in this new environment requires a learning curve. Get the cookbooks if you must, search online or invent your own recipes. Either way, how you go about cooking will be different than at home.

My favorite meal on the road is made from four ingredients. Lisa invented this meal because that's all the food we had on the rig at the time.

What were the ingredients?

Half a jar of olives, an onion, a box of pasta, and a can of crushed tomatoes.

What's the recipe?

Chop and fry one onion until clear, add a can of crushed tomatoes or chop up some fresh tomatoes, and add the half jar of olives. Let it simmer. Use that as the sauce for your cooked pasta. The taste blew my mind.

Grilling always tastes great. A portable gas grill is cheap and handy. There are many small types. I like the Weber tabletop model. We bought our first propane tabletop grill at a garage sale for $5 and it lasted three years. A propane grill is a tad space-consuming, but it can be stored for travel outside, even if latched onto the roof. A grill takes advantage of the propane you'll carry anyway.

TIP: When you have electricity, for everything from burgers to veggies, you can't beat a George Foreman grill. The small model is easy to find at thrift stores.

Use any grill like George's for fresh veggies such as zucchini. This one, or an equivalent grill, is small, easy to store and use, inside or outside. It cooks well. We've had several and each one was bought used for next to nothing.

The other handy device we discovered later in our travels when plugged in, is an electric tabletop induction cooker. Like the George Foreman Grill, it doesn't take much space. It uses 110-V power and works extremely well due to its ability to control temperature precisely. To use a tabletop cooker like this one you must have induction-compatible cookware. Like with George Foreman and tabletop grills, check thrift stores for all the induction pans you need. You might find a cooker, too. Inductive cookware can also be used on the stove or campfire as well. One set of pots does it all if the right kind. Don't worry about fancy brands or remembering materials that are okay to use. Here is a simple trick. If the pot is magnetic, it will work on induction.

Plus, induction cookers readily accept Grandma's cast iron cookware. Although heavy, cast-iron cooks beautifully, even over a campfire.

When we are sitting long-term, we take a portable electric oven. To be frank, standard RV ovens, new or old, suck. Our portable is electric, but some use liquified petroleum (LP) gas. In our experience, RV ovens make the indoors unbearably hot and they don't work well besides. They're only usable in winter. They aren't big enough or consistent enough in temperature for meaningful baking. Baking in an RV oven requires modifications to recipes and procedures. But it may be worth the effort — cooking and baking yourself means better living by way of better health. Fresh bread, think of it, smell it in your brain! No preservatives and you don't need them because that bread won't last long.

A good portable oven can do anything a house oven can do; some even have a built-in air-fryer function. Do your research before you buy one. Read the reviews and ask around. Don't expect the one that came with the rig to cut the mustard.

Old-fashioned portable tabletop camp stoves are available new and used. Some work on white gas, some on butane, others on propane. All are fine for weekend campers, but don't bother bringing portable camp stoves along unless you have no other way. One-pound propane bottles and other camp stove fuels are expensive. Fuel in small containers for highly portable stoves and heaters cost a lot more per pound or fluid ounce in small containers.

When we reconfigured our Carriage fifth-wheel, we removed the stock oven/stove and added a two-burner LP gas range top for cheap. Where the oven was is now much-needed cabinet space. We supplement our range with a portable induction cooktop and a portable pizza oven we use outside only and it runs on propane. That pizza oven is amazing!

Carry on board whatever electric cooking devices help you make the food you like most. This might mean a rice cooker, crock pot, George Foreman grill, or induction cooker. Base your selection on what you eat most and what fits best into limited space. These appliances are small, easy to use, work well, and don't use the RV's propane.

TIP: Use the campground's electricity when provided to cook, heat water, and warm the rig to save money on LP gas. Take advantage of full hook-ups.

Bring decent knives and tableware. Plastic forks break and the knives don't cut it. You won't need a lot of cutlery, but good quality means usable. Don't cheap out. If you need to buy something, look for used stuff at thrift stores and garage sales for the best deals, but get what you *need* even if at full price. You can't split firewood or clean fish with a boy scout knife.

Campfire Cooking

Campfire cooking is mad fun. It requires a grill that can be set over the fire and maybe a grill basket for fish or veggies. Treat yourself to at least one good outdoor cooking cookbook.

Firestarter trick: Take a cotton ball and load it with Vicks or Vaseline. Any petroleum jelly, even an antiseptic ointment, will work. Wrap the infused cotton ball in wax paper or a paper towel. That is now a fire-starter. Paper plates are wax-coated and also work for starting fires. Don't waste money on chemical charcoal lighter fluids. They smell bad and pollute the ground and air.

Baked Alaska: Once, as a child, while tent camping in the middle of an isolated state forest, my parents made a baked Alaska — a pound cake hollowed out, stuffed with ice cream, and covered in egg white that gets baked in an oven. The ice cream is insulated, so it doesn't melt. The cake comes out warm and crispy when finished.

How do you do that out in the woods?

You'll need a cast iron Dutch Oven, which is big and heavy and not easy to tote around. It's a great thing for weekend camping, but I wouldn't recommend running out to buy one or lugging one around if you have limited space. They aren't cheap, but they are great when cooking for a big group. We used to make a Dutch Oven Mulligan stew to die for while family camping. Campers wanting to cover a lot of ground should forgo the Dutch Oven.

Propane Management

Cooking options are good to have. Roughing it? Cooking on the campfire is a blast. The electric cookers I mentioned are great when plugged in. It's great to use the campgrounds' power rather than your stored energy resources.

Of course, the rig's propane stove, for most of us, is primary. That stove may be the only option. One can't avoid propane. One must monitor and maintain propane systems for safety.

As for us, we use less propane and more free power when available. Traveling or sitting, liquified petroleum gas (LP) requires close attention. Propane is the most common type of gas. It's what backyard grills use.

> **TIP:** The number one thing you should do with the typical 20-pound LP tank is refill it. Don't swap out empties at a tank exchange center which are those places where you leave an empty tank and buy a full one. That exchange comes with an inflated price. Tank exchanges are only good for replacing a beat-up, crappy tank. Who doesn't like a nice, shiny one?

Propane tanks must be recertified every eight to twelve years depending on state requirements. Every tank has a construction date stamped on it. The places where you get a tank refilled may check the tank's date. If they do and find your tank outdated, they won't refill it. That can be a problem. When people toss their old tanks in the garbage, it's usually for that reason.

Old LP tanks may look bad, but tanks from an exchange center are recertified, so those old ones gotten at an exchange are trustworthy. Why the recertification? There is a valve inside LP tanks that goes bad over time. This device prevents gas from escaping when the tank is not hooked up. For safety, you want that valve to work properly.

Travel trailers and fifth-wheels usually have two removable and refillable LP tanks. 20-pound tanks, the same kind used on a backyard grill, are the most common. 30-pound tanks are typical on big rigs like fifth-wheels. Many motorhomes have a built-in tank which is difficult if not near impossible to remove. No refilling station ever checked the on-board tank's date stamp on our Class-A Mallard.

If you turn in an empty tank every time it's empty, you're losing money. To save money on propane, own your 20 or 30-pound tanks. You'll get a fuller tank at a lower rate per pound at filling stations. Exchange centers often give less LP than the tank will hold and they charge a premium. You can find LP filling stations listed online. You'll be surprised at how many places refill tanks. Refilling stations are common at older gas stations, feed stores, farm equipment sellers, campgrounds, some truck stops, and my favorite place to shop — independently owned and operated hardware stores.

Just remember: If you have outdated 20-lb tanks and the local guy offers to refill them, don't do that! Your safety is at risk. Turn it in at an exchange and get a fresh one.

We live way out in the woods. The feed store one mile up the road refills LP tanks as does the hardware store three miles away. The nearest real town is over 20 miles from here. There are about six tank exchanges within two miles of me but only a few refill locations. Every dollar store has a tank exchange. What none of them will exchange is anything bigger or smaller than a 20-pound tank. Thirty-pound tanks, standard on fifth-wheel rigs, are out of luck at exchange sites.

Most older rigs with 30-pound tanks will likely come with outdated units. Those tanks must be recertified, and that often forces the new owner of the used RV to buy new tanks. We learned recently that it's less expensive to buy a new 30-pound LP tank than it is to have an old one recertified. That may be different where you are.

TIP: Before you buy, check if the LP tanks are current. For safety, keep your tanks fresh. Serious long-term fixed in place RV dwellers can adapt bigger LP tanks, gotten from the local gas suppliers, to provide gas for the rig. These are the same kind of tanks used on regular homes. Buying a large quantity of fuel is cheaper per pound and delivery is often free.

TIP: A few changed gas fittings and any RV can be fed LP gas with a 100-pound tank which holds about 23.5 gallons of propane. Typically, whole house tanks top out at 500 lbs.

Truck-based motorhomes have fixed LP tanks mounted to the frame. You shouldn't need to get a fixed-in-place tank recertified — I've never seen or heard of anyone doing that — but you should test it.

Our 1990 Class-A had an on-board propane tank, 60 pounds (about 12 gallons). We carefully inspected it and declared it good and worthy of preservation. If you aren't sure, get the tank looked at by a professional. As for the tank on our Class-A...

We painfully scraped and ground off the rust with non-sparking hand tools and repainted the tank ourselves. We tested the connections and gas lines for leaks. The tank was good, but we discovered that the way it had been mounted was not good.

Removing that tank required a major effort. We also would have had to make custom suspension bands to put it back in place. Every car's gas tank has easy to get mass-produced steel band straps. RV tank hangers are not off-the-shelf items. RV factories have banding machines. We didn't.

Our solution was to paint it in place. How? We laid on our backs under the rig for days and days scraping and eating rust. It sucked, but we made our tank reliable. Face shields were not optional.

TIP: Before you buy a motorhome with a built-on LP tank inspect its condition.

If you buy a rig from a dealer, force them to guarantee the propane tank. With on-board tanks, you normally drive the rig to the propane station. If you aren't ever going to move the rig, abandon the on-board tank and go direct. A rented tank is the best option if the rig won't move.

TIP: Some propane companies that service mobile home parks will also refill motorhomes.

That's how we filled our Class-A when we didn't want to drive out. You can stop the LP delivery truck driver when he's in the park and ask. I've had propane drivers take my order on the spot.

As to working on and checking gas fittings yourself, plumbing-skilled people should understand the particulars. If that ain't you, get a knowledgeable person to look before you buy. Get a written warranty.

TIP: Wherever the portable tanks are on a rig you will find rubber hose connections. Is that rubber line cracked? Dry-rotted? Always check!

This hose, which goes from the tank splitter to the hard pipe connection, is a flexible rubber pipe with regulator and brass ends. That flex-pipe takes a beating and should be checked regularly. This tank-splitter-regulator setup is something you will likely change yourself when it fails, and it will eventually. You won't get a leak inside, but you may lose a tank full of gas before you know it leaked. That happened to us.

You'll need to learn how to test gas connections for leaks, because you'll be connecting and un-connecting propane fittings. You may need to change common fittings and hoses which do go bad. Safe-off your gas systems with regular leak checks.

That may save your life.

TIP: Testing gas connections requires a spray bottle filled with soapy water. Spray the area and watch. If there's a leak, there will be bubbles. Rinse the soap off when finished.

You will change gas hoses and the splitter eventually. Don't be afraid. This is basic plumbing and very simple. Wherever gas connections or fittings are, there is that simple way to test for leaks. *This is important.* You may not smell a gas leak until it's a big problem. Test all your gas fittings inside and outside before you launch.

Even a brand-new rig can have gas leaks and bad detectors from the factory. We can't state strongly enough how important smoke, carbon dioxide, and LP gas detectors are. They don't always work. You must test them. Do this per manufacturer's instructions.

Once while we had a visitor in the Class-C, I accidentally opened one of the stove burners. New to RVs, I expected the burner to light. It didn't have an auto igniter (common with household burners), and I didn't know that. I should have read the instructions. I didn't hear the clicker. I figured the gas was off at the tanks.

Wrong!

The door and windows were open and we sat inside chatting, a trio of happy campers. Our propane detector saved the day! We didn't smell gas until the place was inundated. We quickly went outside and were lucky the place didn't blow sky-high.

Roof Air Conditioning

You may have noticed rigs going down the road with a streamlined box on the roof. That's a roof-mounted air conditioning unit, and they suck. Most rigs, even some pop-up campers, come with a roof air unit or two. They cost a lot to replace when, not if, they go bad. RV roof air units are not rechargeable like a car or home heating-and-cooling system (HVAC).

However, roof airs can be repaired, unless they leak coolant. If it leaks, it's done.

Everywhere I go in Florida, I see standard house window air conditioning units hanging out of rig windows although they have a roof air. You see window units on RVs because when a roof air stops working, people assume it's toast and abandon it. Replacement cost is many times more than a home unit. Not to mention that these roof units weigh 80 to 120 pounds. Taking one off the roof is no picnic. I know, I've done it myself.

What people don't know is that RV roof air conditioning units aren't hard to fix, unless they start leaking coolant. It's near impossible to find anyone willing to work on a roof mounted air unit regardless of the issue. Fixing it, if it can be fixed, is likely up to you. The good news is — it's not that hard to do if you have basic mechanical skills and can understand the directions.

Other than the unrepairable closed coolant system, you only have a handful of parts: A control board, starting capacitors, a fan motor, and electrical connections. One bad ground wire and your unit won't run. When the roof air conditioning unit takes a dump, it might be worth troubleshooting. YouTube is your friend here. Even so, you might decide to give up on it anyway.

Roof air units cost a lot for something so inefficient. Many employ ducts in the ceiling (or occasionally floors) so they run quieter. That's good and bad. Ducted units require a higher capacity fan and greater BTU output to push cold air through the ceiling cavity which is always much hotter than exterior ambient temperature.

Our fifth-wheel rig needs 15,000 BTUs to get the job done. It struggled in Florida. The replacement unit, which would be more efficient than the original due to newer technology, cost way more than $1,000, and that's without installation — not to mention, we couldn't find anybody willing to do the work.

To rectify this on the fifth-wheel, we eliminated the roof unit and bought two house-type window units at 6,000 BTU each. Not only do the two small room units do a better job, we use less power and we don't need to run both of them all the time. In cost and efficiency, the window units are far better, cheaper and easier to replace.

To be fair, before we gave up on the Carriage's roof air we fixed it a few times, such as replacing capacitors and a new fan motor but she was getting weak with age so when it took a big dump, we changed gears.

When an older used rig comes with a roof air unit that works, keep using that system. When it fails, consider window units. Our 1978 Class-C came with a roof air and it never failed or needed parts because it was hardly ever used and they made them better back then. We had the same experience with our Class-A as with the fifth-wheel. The air worked well on the Class-A but we eventually had to replace the capacitors, fan motor and control board at different times. Air conditioning runs constantly in Florida summers.

In our Sunline, Class-A and C, the air wasn't ducted. Older rigs, large or small, trailer based or truck based, generally do not use ductwork. Ductwork is less common on smaller rigs like our Sunline. Non-ducted roof air is noisy, more so than a window unit. A window air doesn't need to work as hard as a ducted unit and so may last longer.

TIP: When buying a used rig, test the air conditioning. Also note if there's any place where a window unit will fit. We added breakers and outlets to plug in our window units. Our electric bill has decreased remarkably.

Speaking of keeping cool, most rigs come with a powered roof-mounted vent-fan or two. These are similar to a bathroom fan but stronger. They are typically 12-volt. These ceiling vents do a good job moving air. Replacements are available at a reasonable price. Running the roof fan (Not the roof air's fan) with opened windows works well to moderate interior temperatures, barring high humidity. These fans eat batteries! Be careful with them while boondocking. Keep an eye on the voltage meter.

House Utilities

Your RV will be equipped with redundant utility systems designed to hook up to campground sewer, power, and water. Redundant systems provide the same services when not hooked up. This dual nature of RVs allows boondocking.

Electricity: Electrical systems include both high-voltage, 110-volt house current and low-voltage, 12-volt power like a car. The 110-volt system operates the microwave, air conditioner, and any normal 110 appliance. These appliances only work while you are plugged in or running a generator. The 12-volt system operates some lighting, water pump, heating system controls, roof fan, water heater controls, stove exhaust fan, refrigerator controls, and built-in gas detectors. The 12-volt system relies on your house batteries. It is wise to keep batteries well-charged in case of a power outage.

TIP: If your rig doesn't already have two house batteries, add another one if you can.

Batteries: RV and marine deep-well house batteries ain't cheap. Be warned it doesn't pay to use anything but the best deep-well you can. Research batteries online for the best deals and warranties.

We like acid glass mat batteries also known as "AGM" batteries. They don't need to vent and are safer than the old-fashioned, lead-acid batteries. Plus, an unused glass mat battery does not need a battery tender when stored for a year or more. When not in use, a glass mat will not discharge more than a few percent.

Solar Vs. Battery: Commonly, campers use solar panels to change batteries. Boondockers without generators have no other power source. They may use power inverters to run 110-volt devices from the 12-volt source. This technique eats juice quickly, which requires more batteries. Have I mentioned batteries aren't cheap? And they're heavy! Yet, for boondocking, more is better.

We have found that it's not practical and too costly to live on solar and batteries alone long-term. Extra batteries are good, but living on batteries doesn't get our seal of approval unless you are totally off-grid and have no other way. For long-term, off-grid living, solar power is a viable option but sucky if you need 110-V power and haven't got massive power storage.

The refrigerator will be a dual system (some are three-way) running on either 110-volt electric or a combination of 12-volt and propane. Therefore, as long as you have batteries and gas, the refrigerator stays cold. While boondocking, this is how you live. Run out of batteries or liquified petroleum, go and get a cooler and some ice, quick. Or eat all your food. Three-way refrigerators also work on 12-volt directly, but they eat batteries fast.

Remember: If you smell ammonia, your refrigerator coolant is leaking. That leak cannot be repaired.

I'm not kidding when I say RV refrigerators are way, way expensive. When the two-way in our Carriage died, we replaced it with a regular apartment-size house unit. Why? The RV refrigerator cost $1400 while the house unit cost 200 bucks with 20% more room inside it. This fifth-wheel ain't going nowhere. She's a tiny-house now. Mobile rigs must have the 2 or 3-way RV type. It's the only thing that makes sense. How'd I get a new refrigerator so cheap? My VA discount plus more money off for the small dent it had. Score!

12-volt also powers your furnace fan and is used to operate the furnace and water heater's control boards. These devices can run without 110-V but can't run without 12-volt power. How these work is pretty simple. Your RV should come with a booklet telling you which brand/type of utility devices you have and how to operate them. If you don't have the manufacturer's paperwork, no problem. Download a PDF. Some parts do go bad. There aren't many parts, but most are easily replaced. When the heat stops working, don't panic. It can be fixed. We recently replaced the fan motor on our furnace. Simple to do but a pain in the ass.

Hot water: Typically, older RVs have a six-gallon hot water heater tank. Newer units may have the 10-gallon option. I know six gallons doesn't sound like much water, and it isn't. But it *is* plenty for a shower. Because of the low holding capacity of RV hot water (HW) heaters, water reheats fast. Modern rigs generally have an electric heating element wand inside the HW tank to supplement the gas-fired feature. These heater wands require 110-volts. You don't need LP gas when you're plugged in. If you have an older rig without the electric wand, you can add one. They aren't too expensive, and they are easy to install. Buy the kit. Read the instructions. You'll screw the wand into the anode port.

|TIP: Keep an eye on the hot water heater anode and change it as needed.

What's an anode? It's a removable metal rod inside your HW tank which is designed to rot instead of your tank walls. It's a sacrificial piece of weak metal that will be attacked first by way of electrolysis to prevent or slow erosion of the tank's steel walls. Hot water tanks are either steel or aluminum. The aluminum ones (Atwood usually) last longer and don't rust. Steel tanks do not last as long so keeping up on the anode is critical. Every three to five years, remove and inspect the anode. Better yet, check it when you do your annual flush-out of the water heater. Yes, another chore to stay on top of. HW tanks collect mineral sediment just like your motor's radiator so be sure to filter your water.

HW heater parts can be replaced with relative ease. Repairable parts include the control board, tank thermostat, anode, electrical connections, pressure relief valve, and propane burners.

Potable water: An RV's water system includes a freshwater holding tank for potable water and a 12-volt pump to deliver it. Rigs also have a direct connection for city water to supply the house while hooked up. Depending on the rig, you may have the capacity to carry 30 to 80 gallons of fresh water. Water tanks require occasional anti-germ maintenance as we explained above. The entire house system will need draining and winterizing before storing, depending on climate.

> **TIP:** It is advisable to keep a good supply of water on-board at all times, especially during hurricane season. Sanitizing the water system should be done at least once a year.

> **TIP:** Wherever you hook up or when filling a freshwater tank, use a sediment filter. Mineralized water is bad for the rig.

Wastewater and dump stations: Wastewater is contained in two holding tanks mounted under the rig. One tank is for *black water* and the other tank is for *gray water*. Most RV parks have sewer hookups. Those that do not have a sewer inlet at the campsite may have a dump station. This is a central location where any rig can pull up, connect to an inlet, and let her rip. In many places, it's legal to dump gray water on the ground. Typically, rigs with outdoor showers spill water on the ground. Willy-nilly gray dumping is considered bad manners. Never do that in a parking lot!

NEVER dump blackwater on the ground!

If you are stationary and have the ability to install regular plumbing, remove your waste tanks. Save them for later reinstalling if you like. Not going to pull your rig? Drop the tanks. Get a house toilet. I'm talking to you snowbirds who leave your rigs at the park permanently.

RV's dual systems allow you to get off the grid and stay there for as long as your supplies and waste tanks hold out. Power outages don't scare us. Speaking of power...

Solar mounting: We mentioned how much we love boondocking in the great outdoors. To that effect, many newer RVs come equipped with roof mounted solar panels as an option. Portable solar is easy to come by at a reasonable price and has kept us flush with battery power for as long as we liked. Permanent roof-mounted solar panels are available, but that brings you back to the discussion on roofs and penetrations, etc.

Any kind of roof mount or penetration is subject to leaks. Our portable suitcase solar kit does the job for us with no installation required.

Generators: Generators often come installed on bigger rigs, especially Class-C, Class-A, and some fifth-wheel trailers. I have mixed feelings about generators. We bought a portable and brought it along in the Class-C, and never used it. We had a nice "low-hours" (meaning hardly-ever used) Onan generator built-in on the Class-A. The Onan brand generator is a bullet-proof two-cylinder and the best of its kind. We never used it.

If you camp in the hot weather and don't have hookups, you will want and need a generator. People that go to the big auto races like Daytona or Poconos Raceway and camp on the infield will need that generator. Generators make a lot of noise. If you're not camping on a race track infield, it might sound like you are. Generators are good for emergencies. You don't need one to keep up the batteries if you have solar. Many older rigs have excellent Onan generators, and most of them were never used. If you need a generator, I would recommend a Japanese brand over a Chinese-made one.

We have two generators at our current home base, one is a 4000W LP and flex-fuel capable unit that can run everything including the A/C. (Flex meaning it can run on LP or gasoline.) The other is a 1300W gas job, good to keep the refrigerator going and recharge the batteries on very little gas. When on the road, we don't haul a generator. We have them at base camp because the power goes out during hurricane season here.

Smart chargers: Speaking of batteries and changing, many older RVs do not have a smart charger. That's a problem because you can overcharge a battery and kill it. Get one if you don't have it. They aren't hard to install. It will replace the old charging interface and manage multi-battery systems far better.

If you have an older truck or one without a tow package, install a battery isolator on the truck to prevent the motor from draining the house batteries and visa-versa. Some setups can also be reversed to start the motor when the house is good and the truck battery is dead. Very handy! Make sure the isolator works. If you don't have one and are parking for a long time, disconnect the truck's battery or unplug the rig from the truck. We have a quick disconnect switch on the van's battery for that.

More on Toads

A toad is a street-legal vehicle you bring along with the house. It's what you tow such as a car on a trailer, a car on a car dolly, a car inside an enclosed trailer, or a car/light truck being towed four wheels on the ground with a towbar.

I will also call any motor vehicle you bring along a "toad" if it isn't the house. Toads can be motorcycles on a trailer or a bumper-mounted lightweight motorcycle, E-bike, or moped. If towing a travel trailer, the truck is a front toad (the part that *towed* the trailer).

Why bring a toad? After making camp you aren't going to break camp to run out for something you need. Once you park, the toad allows you to go sightseeing and supply hunting.

TIP: Preload supplies so you won't *need* to ride out.

Common Toad Methods Pros and Cons

Tow Dolly. We feel that tow dollies aren't the best way to haul cars, although commonly used. Tow dollies can be bought or rented. They're common because they aren't expensive, new or used. There are several brands with different methods for attaching the car. The front wheels of the car go on the dolly and the rear wheels ride on the ground. The dolly is pulled by the rig, usually a big Class-A or big Class-C. Most dollies have a surge break and you want that.

The biggest downside of the dolly is you can't back up, due to the surge brakes. Also, a car on a dolly is not articulated well for backing. This was a big issue for us as you read earlier. The other big downside is that sometimes cars slip off of car dollies. We have seen this going down the road. In another lane, a car was off the dolly and being dragged along by the safety chains. The driver had no idea!

TIP: While towing one must always keep an eye on the toad.

We almost lost a car twice on the same trip because of how the dolly's strapping worked. We later devised/engineered a better method for holding the wheels in place on the dolly.

With dollies, your car's steering must be left unlocked. Thus, your key remains in the ignition switch. This can drain your toad's battery. (A battery disconnect-switch will remedy that.) You'll need portable magnetic tail lights hooked to the rig so the dolly has signal lights. Some setups can tether the car to the rig to allow the toad's lights to work. That costs more, and not every car or rig's wiring can be tapped with ease. Some have built-in brake lights. Car dollies, when they work right, are easy to load, cheaper than a car trailer, easy to store and maintain.

Car Trailers: Car trailers are a good option. They can be enclosed or open. You can back up. Loading isn't bad. The big downside is they aren't cheap. Another downside is they are long. Length could also be considered a benefit, because the longer the trailer, the easier it is to back it up. But, a 30-foot rig hauling a 20-foot car trailer is a long line of stuff you'll need to keep in check, park, and maneuver. A typical car trailer costs more than my rig! Owners of Class-A rigs, especially snowbirds, often tow a car but seldom do we see car trailers.

Four wheels on the ground: This is, in our view, the best way to bring a car along while driving a Class-A or C rig. This is done by way of a towbar. The downside is, again, you can't back up. The good side of that bad side is that unhooking a towbar and re-hooking it takes very little time and effort. Many towbars are self-adjusting and that greatly simplifies hooking up. The bad side is — not all cars can be or should be towed four wheels down. Some cars are designed to allow towing four wheels on the ground, such as many of the old Saturn cars, the older Honda Rav-4, and some Jeeps.

TIP: Before you buy a towbar, make sure your potential toad is towable.

The towbar brackets needed to hook up the car aren't cheap or easy to install. Altogether, it's cheaper than a car trailer and about the same as a dolly. Towbar systems are specific to each car. If you change car brand or type, you'll need a different towbar mount each time.

Note: Any rear-wheel-drive car can be towed with a towbar if you disconnect the drive shaft. Cars with automatic transmissions can't be towed wheels down unless the transmission has a built-in feature to allow for towing. Front-wheel drive cars seldom have that feature. Many transmissions have been destroyed by towing with a towbar. The car's wheels will spin the transmission's internals without circulating fluids properly.

One old-time car that is the easiest to tow because it doesn't require anything special is the Volkswagen Beetle. They are light and their manual transmissions need only be put into neutral. Not so with the VW automatic transmissions. The classic bug and VW-based dune buggies used to be a cheap way to do four-wheel towing. Sadly, old cars have gotten pricey.

Front Toad: That's how you tow a travel trailer. It can be any truck sufficient for your needs. 150-size pickup trucks can handle most travel trailers if the engine has enough horsepower. 250- and 350-sized trucks are the only way to do fifth-wheels. People often overload their front toads. Don't do that. Make sure your truck's towing capacity can handle the weight of your trailer.

Note: Many bigger fifth-wheels are overweight for the 350 trucks people use. *Check legal requirements before you tow.* The downside of the big truck is you're stuck with a big truck. You have big truck fuel consumption and repair costs. On the plus side, big powerful trucks pull way better than undersized trucks. Towing a travel trailer with a 350 truck is a breeze. You'll appreciate that gas-sucking truck motor should you hit the mountains.

Look into stabilizer bars if you tow a long and heavy travel trailer. Tongue weight is critical. The load must be balanced correctly or the trailer will wiggle and cause a jackknife. Stabilizer bars help reduce or prevent trailer sway.

The one plus about towing a fifth-wheel is they are easier to control because the weight is balanced over the truck's rear axle. They are responsive and easier to maneuver into tight spots. Better balancing means less chance of jackknifing. There is a reason why most snowbirds in this park and everywhere we've been are fifth-wheel dwellers. It's easier to park and haul one barring the fact they are tall making head room a problem.

Our Take on Toads: We have used dollies and trailers and lusted for a four-wheels-on-the-ground towbar setup but never got there. While on the road full-time, the motorcycles were our toads. For the way we traveled, the bikes were the best solution except when it was cold. We kept our setup light so we could pick up and go with ease. Our street-legal dirt bikes got us into places others could not go. Sitting more long-term, the bikes didn't do it for us anymore. That's when we switched to the Class-A and car dolly combination as we eventually only traveled seasonally.

Now that we are base camped, we created a different setup for touring. We have a 1996 van and haul a Sunline travel trailer. The van is convertible and has tons of extra storage. The Sunline's got everything necessary for a long stay. We go to north in the summer months and it's fine for that. When we tour again, we will use this setup.

The Sunline is short and easy to back up as it's about the same overall length as the van. We could go back on the road indefinitely with the Sunline. The van doesn't get great gas mileage while towing, but it's not bad otherwise. The only hiccough is the van has a 302 motor, and that makes it underpowered for the mountains, but we manage. At some point, we may put a 351 motor in it or replace the van with a more powerful one. Newer motors get better gas mileage compared to our old van and new engines also have more horsepower for the same size. Because we got the van to use as a bug-out vehicle, we didn't anticipate towing with it. The van is great for sleeping in while on a long commute. The bug-out van also allows us to get out fast to dodge incoming storms with or without the Sunline. When it comes to front toads, we think vans are the best option for their extra storage capacity. Plus, vans are always less expensive than equivalent weight capacity pickup trucks. Pickups are popular, vans aren't.

We do love a bargain, don't we.

SECTION FOUR:

Final Considerations

The RV American Dream

We hope you tasted the flavors and realities of living the RV life. This guide was intended to help you decide if this lifestyle will work for you.

Perhaps you'll try it and at some point, go back to house living or, like us, stay permanently in an RV/mobile home park. Living the RV way doesn't suit everyone.

If you are young and chasing the American dream, living in an RV may seem like a failure. To some people living this way represents a defeat. We disagree. It feels like a step away from their dreams whereas RVing can help one get there...For some, the ability to do this *is* the dream.

People work-camp for whatever reason. We see full-time working gypsies a lot. They move in for six months and are gone, according to their desires. That's a good dreamscape in our view.

I lost track of how many RV dwellers came to this park, stayed a few years, and wound up getting a house. Living in an RV was way cheaper than what they likely came from, yet they didn't stay. They saved enough money to move on, I guess.

Coming and going is one of the trends we've seen firsthand. We've also seen the opposite. One woman who settled here in a house wanted back on the road and traded her house, a real house, for a Class-A and hit the road. We've seen a lot of people coming and going. This mixed park of RVs, houses, and trailer homes reinvents itself each season.

Another big trend we see happening a lot is this. People sell the house, get the RV, drive a while, stay longer and longer at a wintering spot, and then go on to buy a single-wide trailer or a house because they like the place where they landed and connected with the people there. That's fine with us.

As for us, we will stick with having wheels under us. Our observation is that the snowbirds come for the amenities and to escape from the cold. They come back or stay to live here because of the people they meet. Have I mentioned camping people, as a lot, are friendly and helpful? They come, they see, they stay.

What better way is there to look around and figure out where you want to be other than to RV around the nation? Why not drive all over the place and see it for yourself?

That's what we did.

It's good to go exploring. Do it with open eyes and adjustable expectations.

We created a home base here that followed the typical pattern. We wintered here a few times and saw the advantages. Mostly, we liked the community and still do. So, we moved into snowbird/summerbird mode for a few years to try the place out. That eventually led to planting ourselves here. We stayed for many reasons, and it's inexpensive! Yet we maintain the ability to hit the road. We gypsy types always keep one foot outside of the door.

What kind of American Dreamers are RV-happy?

People who don't worry about status, who see the park-home/mobile home/RV as a boon and not a detriment or a symbol of failure. If the American dream, for you, is to live a peaceful, quiet, less expensive, simpler life, the RV life might be what you are looking for. If you love the outdoors, are active, and don't mind fixing things, and learning things, this will work for you.

Before jumping into the RV life, it is good to know what your dream is. One should consider if the dream is realistic, what it takes to get there, what it costs, and whether it's worth it. If you choose this life, as we have, that can be a very good thing.

It should not be a secret to you that wages have been stagnant for the last 40 years, prices keep rising, and the cost of housing has made the American dream of home ownership all but impossible for many folks. Lots of people, myself included, faced unexpected life and financial changes forcing us into a low-income situation. If you get a rig before that happens, you will never be homeless. It's always good to have a back-up plan! If you never *need* to live as we do, God bless. Then, go camping and have fun. Consider your rig an insurance policy.

Base Camp and Tiny Houses:

These days we live in a 34-foot Carriage brand fifth-wheel in a mixed RV/mobile home park within the middle of a national forest in Florida. Living this way is cheap as dirt compared to where we lived previously. We paid $5,000 for this rig and did extensive remodeling. We made this rig into a great tiny house. And, we have the short Sunline and van for trips. From here, we can go anywhere.

When not here, because we are on wheels and not fixed to the ground, the park allows us to pay a small storage fee. We can leave for up to six months without paying full rent. We're still living the RV life but with a real address at base camp. We summered in Florida a few times to test and see if we would adapt. We did but we don't always stay the summer. The road calls and so we go. The Sunline is our home when away, no matter where we park it.

Here is a summary of what we did to our fifth-wheel. We put on an iron roof, remodeled the kitchen, eliminated the roof air and skylights (for leak prevention), ripped out the carpets and installed laminate floors, sheet-rocked the ceilings, dumped the (deceased) RV refrigerator for a larger capacity, house refrigerator, removed the waste tanks and installed regular house plumbing.

In effect, we made it into a tiny house. This is the cheap way to have a tiny house. Take an old rig and update it. We have upgraded every rig we've had and it paid off at resale time. With these improvements, this old rig is now worth more, and is easier to sell if we ever need to.

We have an enclosed storage trailer, the Sunline, the van, and a car. Everything we have can roll out of here if this park fails. We always have one foot out the door, no matter where we are. Shit happens. Park owners come and go. Hurricanes threaten, but that doesn't scare us. Bad weather coming? We hook up and go. Insurance covers the house's contents should a mishap strike. We are prepared to lose everything and start over. This is tiny house living at its best.

What about the tiny house movement?

As a construction expert, I have issues with the tiny houses I've seen online and in person. Most of them are fire traps and overbuilt on overstressed trailers. Built just like a house means they're too heavy for the trailers they're typically built on. The right capacity trailer prices such homes out of reach. They look nice with fancy woodwork and clever designs, but they aren't safe, in my view, and typically lack storage. It costs a lot of money to have someone move one. You can't haul one easily any distance yourself and moving it may well need permits and an escort service.

A tiny house is just like the old-time seasonal bungalows that were once common in shore towns and lakesides. I don't see any advantages in buying one. Before you buy a tiny house, have an expert look at it. Tiny house builders aren't required to follow home construction standards or codes!

Same with rig manufacturers but they do have industry standards.

We could write a book about building a tiny house and the ideal travel trailer but this ain't about that. Don't get caught up in the tiny house craze. Do the homework necessary to understand what you are looking at should you decide to go with a tiny house. What is a tiny house anyway? It's small and you live in it just like an RV. Why pay double for the same or less space?

To Park or Not

Full-timer-to-be, be warned. You will park a lot. You will need to winter somewhere be it Florida, Arizona, Texas, or some other southern location. Staying in the cold northern climate requires extensive winterization which gets costly. If you want to save money and enjoy life, you will park. Where, when, and how long depends on how things fall out for you and what you evolve into needing and wanting. You may start by flying hither and yon. That only works if well-prepared. Expect plans to change. Expect your expectations to prove good and bad. You may not expect to park long term, but you will.

Why anticipate long-term sitting?

RVing is an evolutionary process. No matter how much you study, make lists, and prepare before launching, things crop up. Not everything is on the list. Long-term parking strategies should be on that list. Before launch, some of what you thought you'd need isn't needed. Maybe what you loaded ain't practical. What you didn't want you didn't take but later needed. Things change as you go. Needs must supersede wants.

For example, I had a lighted makeup mirror in the Class-C. It took up a lot of room. I wrongly justified it. I like to keep my eyebrows just so. A stick-on suction cup magnifying mirror, one-tenth the size, works just as well. It fits in my handbag. I'll pluck at a gas station if needs be. Makeup? Nobody wears makeup in a campground. I haven't plastered my face in years but my eyebrows are spot on. I sold the makeup mirror at a campground garage sale.

With small-space-living needs come first, like it or not. Some of the things you brought along aren't going to work. Grandma's big pan might get traded away while traveling and its loss mourned while parked. Don't worry, every thrift shop has a duplicate. Some of the things you decided you won't need; you'll need when sitting. Get what you need when you need it and unload the rest if the plan is to cover distance. Don't get attached to things.

About parking, know thyself and be ready to change your habits. Sitting requires things that flying fast doesn't. When you sit, you will accumulate. Gather only what you don't mind leaving behind. Sitting out the winter with more comfort is fine, but don't get used to collecting if you plan to travel. Sitting puts on RV fat. *Overloaded RVs aren't safe.*

You will find the balance. For us, at first, the plan was to save money while traveling and we did. That meant a lot of free boondocking and moving every week or two. Rare paid-camp stays were done where it was cheap and when the budget allowed. Free Army Corps of Engineers or Bureau of Land Management camps and the like were the usual. Drive-some, sit-some turned out to be our hopscotch way to cover a lot of ground cheaply. Add gas, and camp fees which we avoided more often than not, and we spent *half* of what the apartment cost us.

We never drove more than 300 miles in a day. Most trips between sittings were under 150 miles. Slow and steady sees all. We boondocked our way to and from camps. It wasn't unusual to take a month to cover 300 miles depending upon costs and local points of interest.

Needs and goals change. We evolved and discovered what worked for us. We invented tricks to save money. We got the most out of every buck. When it got too cold, we were ready. One must be prepared. You may be a fair-weather camper chasing the sun and expect golden warmth, but expect the unexpected. Pack cold weather gear anyway!

While leaving Las Vegas heading back east, the desert was warm. No jackets required. The plan was to take Interstate 40 over the high pass. We left at 6 p.m., thinking we'd arrive on the other side a few hours later to boondock. That trip took six hours. We met a blizzard on the high pass. Thirty miles an hour in blinding snow was all I could manage.

Nowhere to stop.

Several big rigs passed us but not another headlight all night. Visions of driving over a cliff haunted me. What I didn't expect was a blizzard or how well the rig handled in the snow — stable as a rock. We never expected a white-out in May.

Being prepared for travel doesn't prepare you for everything. Had we fallen off a cliff that night and landed on a shelf, we could have stayed for weeks on our supplies and cold weather gear.

I'm glad we didn't have to park that way. You may think you will never be stuck in the wilds but be ready for it.

Our Motorhome Gypsy Philosophy

We aren't like the old European concept of gypsies. We aren't traveling around fortune telling, playing three-card Monty, and ripping people off. There are modern bad-guy gypsy-types known as travelers and that ain't us. Many "travelers" are contractors who move into an area, put on crappy roofs, or install diluted driveway sealer, and other scams. Travelers take the money and run before poop hits the fan.

I saw travelers coating the local supermarket parking lot. I told the store manager he was getting ripped off. The heavy kerosene-smell abated after a few weeks and that new finish washed away…as predicted.

We motorhome gypsies aren't like that.

All kinds of people live the motorhome life for all kinds of reasons. We have rarely seen criminal activities while traveling and camping. Camping people are good people by and large.

Who are motorhome gypsies?

We are work campers, retired or disabled people, camp hosts, and adventurers. Some of us have a little bit of money tucked away, most are living hand-to-mouth as are much of the population. Many of us just like being free. We don't want a mortgage and credit card debts dragging us down. A lot of motorhome gypsies see this as the best way to live. We live cheap, smart, and honest. We get by with less. We thrive and make the most of everything. We enjoy the natural world.

As I wrote this, I looked out of the window to see an American Bald Eagle sitting on a dock rail 200 yards away at the lake. That beats the hell out of watching TV.

Campgrounds are the one place where old hippies and rednecks see eye-to-eye. Both types camp for the same reasons. Peace and quiet, campfires, sitting around sipping fuzzy apple juice, shooting the breeze and strumming the old guitar. What can be better?

We love the great outdoors. We marvel over a clear night without light pollution. We seek and find what others miss. We are explorers, adventurers, and seekers with a welcoming eye open for the unexpected. We love to see and learn new things.

We do things for ourselves. We create new ways of cooking, new ways of living, and new ways of seeing what is in front of us. After the wilderness, a blade of grass jetting up out of a city sidewalk crack will jump into one's awareness. Childhood wonder returns. Remember the first shiny rock you found, or that piece of driftwood, or that favorite stick you played with as a child?

We get to do that. We find new and interesting things off the beaten path.

Motorhome gypsies make new paths.

How do we travel? With ease. We hear of interesting places and go. We decide what's next by way of an old map showing forgotten places. We don't go where everybody goes when everybody goes there. We don't follow the crowd. We prefer the middle of nowhere. We like how nowhere feels!

Everywhere is home.

The only question is how long to stay here or there.

Wintering is necessary for most of us, and we have many options and cost considerations on that. When it comes to travel, we trust the wind to blow us where our hearts wish to go. As for us, we'll ride the winds. That's how we find what the others miss. Our brothers and sisters of the road will gladly share the wisdom they acquired with you. We are the world's most spread-out family tribe and you are welcome to join us.

Conclusion

Nothing is permanent for us. Living the motorhome gypsy life has given us new perspectives you can't get by watching television. You have seen some of the problems we encountered along the road. But do you know what? We would do it all again and it ain't over yet. We thought we knew what we were getting into and we prepared for it, but nothing can prepare you for the joys, wonders, and surprises you will find in this life.

By now your head is dancing with visions of mule deer and starry nights. That is good. Before you jump, test the lifestyle. Camp a little. Rent a Class-C. Borrow a rig. Try it.

CheapRVLiving is a YouTube channel whereby this old guy living the life interviews all kinds of full-time Van and RV dwellers, people who make do and come up with clever solutions. Take a look at what free camping people are doing in Quartzsite, Arizona. Quartzsite alone is a world unto itself. Lots of great tips and encouragement is free for the taking on this and many other RV channels.

It is good you read this book. Don't stop here. The best way to try out the motorhome gypsy life is to live it. Get out and look around. The trend is baby boomers are retiring and heading south, but why stop there?

Florida can be just the beginning if you want it to be.

APPENDIX

Big Loop Itinerary

The following is one big trip. The Four Corners loop actually started from Texas as that is when and where we decided to do the Corners. Before the first date below, we were in Pennsylvania, and stopped at Big Meadows Federal Park, Virgina on the Sky Line Drive for the second time. From there we were in a campground near Mayberry, North Carolina and after that on to Florida.

2010

May 5: Camped in Daytona, Fla. to visit Rachel's son. From there we camped near Ocala, Fla. before leaving on.

May 16: Little Rock, Ark. (This might be wrong)

May, 27: A state or federal park called Highlands, in La. or Miss. (We think La.)

June 7: Deep Springs State Park in north Mississippi.

June 11: heading back to Pa. Overheating. Stopped in Ohio at the bicycle museum.

July 15: going back to Florida stopped, on the Sky Line Drive and at a hotel in N.C.

July 21: to about Aug., first Visiting in Ocala, Fla. and went to Key West.

Aug. 7: Back in Pa. Sold the Class-C. Got the Class-A. Added another motorcycle.

Aug. 31: Making ready to leave and loading the new old bike, Honda XL185.

Sept 1: At my sister's house in N.J. repairing the Class-A? Maybe not

Oct 13: Camping on Sky Line Drive, Va. primitive camping.

Oct 16: Skin Line Live Big Meadows federal camp. First time there.

Oct 17: Touring Blue Ridge Mountains on Sky Line Drive onto the Blue Ridge Parkway.

Oct 18: Stuck on the mountain with faded breaks leaving the Blue Ridge Parkway.

Oct. 20: Reached the great Smoky Mountains National Park off the Blue Ridge Parkway.

Oct. 21: Great Smokey Mountains National Park.

Oct. 23: Great Smoky Pilot Ridge Overlook, Blue Ridge Parkway camped several primitive parks.

Oct. 26: Camped private owned park in north Ga. mountains and hills.

Oct. 30: Meet up with Jason in Atlanta boondocking there and on the way south.

Nov. 12: Florida, again. Lake Okeechobee commercial campground about 5 days.

Nov. 18: Florida, Key West with the RV but it's the class -C.

Nov. 25: Ocala, Fla. Visit a State Park.

Dec. 10: Going west on I-10.

Dec. 4–6 : Lake Pontchartrain, New Orleans and the French Quarter.

Dec. 12: Sam Houston National Forest, Texas. Rachel is injured on the bike.

Dec. 13–18: working our way through Texas going south boondocking stops.

Dec. 18–29: 2010 several boondocking stops

Dec. 30: Arrive Aransas Pass, Texas, to winter.

2011

Feb. 1: First week of Feb. we start moving north. The Four Corners Loop begins

Feb. 16: Campground on a river, nice place private owned. Not sure where in Texas.

Feb. 18 to 20 or 21: Another Texas private park. Empty, nice recreation hall. New parking lot park just opened.

Feb. 23: Going north heading out of Texas, long barren ride from flat-lands to hill country.

Feb. 24: Fort Stockton, Texas. Crappy town. Good museum. Gay guy cuts Rachel's hair.

Feb 28: On the road. A long, long road leaving Texas and boondocked.

March 1: Carlsbad Caverns, N.M.

March 3: Roswell, N.M. (This may be wrong.)

March 2: Cibola National Forest, camping near the town of Captain, N.M.

March 5–7: Three Rivers Petroglyph Site. Free campsite.

March 8–9: Desert landscapes fantastic, boondocking.

March 10: Albuquerque, N.M. Petroglyph National Monument was shit but camping at Enchanted Trails RV Park and Trading Post was great.

March 11: Enter El Malpais National Park. Camp at the Ice Cave private owned volcanic park and museum.

March 12–14: El Morro National Monument and the gay campground, Ancient Way.

March 14: Painted Desert and Petrified Forest National Reserves, Ariz.

March 15: Crystal Forest Campground and Painted Desert and Petrified Forest, Ariz.

March 16: Arrive Canyon De Chelly National Monument, Ariz. on native American land.

March 17: Leaving De Chelly. Amazing desert pictures in Ariz. heading to Farmington.

March 17, 18, or 19: Limping into Farmington, N.M. for repairs, UFO story, model train campsite.

March 20: Heading for Mesa Verde High Pass and snow Colorado

March 20: Arrive Mesa Verde, Colo.

March 21–22: Manti-La Sal National Monument. High desert, fantastic landscapes, Colo. into Utah.

March 23: On the road in the snow. Desert pictures.

March 24: Arrive Moab, Utah. Commercial campground.

March 25: First tour of Arches National Park

March, 26: Stay one night in Arches. HC spot open. Not sure of date

March 26 to about April 1?: Toured along Colorado River on bikes and Horse Head Canyon National Park. Camped at Horse Head, N.M.

April 2: Leaving Four Corners in to N.M., and later Nev.

April 4–6: Zion

April 8–9: On I-40 leaving Nev. into Ariz. on High Pass. Hit the blizzard, on the 10th, a sandstorm

April 12: Tucumcari, N.M. Best dinosaur museum ever!

April 16: Petrified Forest of Mississippi, private campground — return to Fla. canceled.

April 18: Barber Motorcycle Museum, Alabama

April 21: Private campground in N.C.

May 3: Back in Pa., closed the Big Loop.

June 10: Sold small bikes. Got big street bikes and MC trailers. Make ready to launch.

Aug. 6: Car show in Pa. with Angel in Macungie, Pa.

Oct. 13: Back in the Shenandoah Valley, Blue Ridge Parkway, Big Meadows. Long stay in the area.

Nov. 17: First time at Lake Bryant, later to become our home base.

Important dates below.

2012

April 26: Bought the Class-A Mallard

May 11: In N.J. at Mary's house fixing the rig

Aug. 6: Class-A ready to roll

Oct. 10: Van dwellers meet-up

Oct. 19: Car dolly problems

Oct, 27: Back to Florida to winter with Saturn car

Glossary

Disclaimer: *These terms and names listed below are commonly used colloquially and may not reflect official or technical terminologies. These are our definitions which are not borrowed or quoted from on-line sources but are normally spoken and understood by campers.*

2- and/or 3-Way Refrigerator: Special made for RVs they can operate without hook-ups by way of two or three on-board utility systems, i.e.: 110-volt power by generator, 12-volt power in some cases by batteries, and propane gas. Note: 12-volt must be available to operate the control board or the refrigerator cannot work. While hooked-up, the 110-volt system is the default.

Access Pass: A federally issued pass card that allows holders free access and or discounts to many federal paid-to-use points of interest. Seniors, veterans and disabled people qualify for this pass.

Air Bags: Supplemental aftermarket suspension devices used to strengthen a weak existing suspension's capacity, stability, and ride height under load. They are adjustable by way of inflated air.

Airport Van: These are extra-long van bodied vehicles used as shuttles by airports and churches. Retired airport vans are often a good value and sought out by van dwellers for home-built campers.

Black Water Tank: Or black tank, a self-contained on-board waste holding tank for toilet waste.

BLM (Bureau of Land Management): The Federal Parks system, National Monuments, Federal Forests, Army Corps of Engineering (Army Corps for short), National Reserves

Boondocking: This is camping without hook-ups and relying on on-board systems. Boondocking usually refers to free overnight parking, such as in truck stops and box store parking lots. One can also boondock at paid locations such as BLM primitive camping areas with or without designated campsites.

Brake Controller: A device used to control the brakes of a towed trailer which is installed on the truck that is doing the towing. These are aftermarket and need to be added unless provided in a factory installed tow-package.

Bunkhouse Camper/RV: Any RV can have a bunkhouse but usually found in travel trailers, which are a small room with bunk beds. Often converted into a walk-in closet.

Bus: Bus usually refers to very large Class-A campers built on a bus chassis or made out of a bus such as a Greyhound or city bus. Rock and roll tour buses are a good example, such as Willie Nelson's rig.

Camp Host: A volunteer who hosts campgrounds and performs light duties in exchange for a free campsite and sometimes other amenities are provided by the park. Most federal campgrounds use a camp host. Some commercial and private camps do as well.

Camper: Usually refers to a travel trailer but can also refer to a pop-up style camper or a pickup truck's removable slide-in camper or anything converted into a camper's configuration. Camper is a general term often used as shorthand for any rig type. The words rig and camper are interchangeable. Camper also means people who camp or go camping.

Campsite/Lot: Refers to paid or free camping locations where the rig is parked for camping.

Car Dolly: Is a towing device whereby the front wheels of the toad are lashed onto a two-wheel trailer/dolly while the rear tires remain on the pavement.

City Water: Refers to any fresh water hook up spigots that is derived from a provided source.

Class-A Motorhomes: These are bus-like motorhomes ranging for 21 to 35 feet long typically, and built on a box truck chassis such as the P-30 truck and others. These can be front mounted gas engines or rear mounted diesel motors. Rear motor variations are known as pushers or diesel pushers and have a heavier chassis.

Class-B Motorhome: These are built on any brand of high-top vans from the mid-1970s until the sprinter vans took over in the late 90s. Extra-long high-top vans have full utilities that are typical in larger rigs. Tight interior space best suited for one person. These rigs are pricey and, in our view, offer no advantages other than being 'stealthy'.

Class-B+: The B-plus is usually based on a Sprinter van truck frame with full utilities and gives more interior space than the standard Class-B. They often have a cab-over section not used for a bed, but for storage. They are expensive and don't have any significant gas saving advantages.

Class-C Motorhome: The C stands for cab-over. Usually based on a 350-size truck from 19 to 32 feet long. These are self-contained with all available utility features. The driving compartment is a van cab in older models. Rare, but sometimes the Class-C is built with a pickup truck cab. Some expensive types are built on 450 trucks and larger trucks such as the Freightliner brand truck.

Commercial Campgrounds: Owned by corporations and are often chain operations with more than one location.

Conversion Rigs: Anything can be made into a camper such as retired ambulances, sprinter vans, high-top and standard vans, hearses, box trucks, enclosed utility trailers, school bus, delivery truck, bread truck, milk truck, and whatever you can think of.

Double Wide: Same as a single wide but they arrive on site in two parts and are joined together on the long plain and finished in the manor of a modular home.

Dump Station: Is a location where an RV can expel or dump the contents of on-board waste tanks. RV parks that do not have individual sewer pipe hook-up inlets on each site often provide a dump station whereby one can relieve the wastes on the way out or into the park. Dump Stations can sometimes be found in truck stops and some camp stores to use for a small fee. Some campgrounds will let you dump for a fee if you are not camping there on site.

Engine Cover: An interior box that covers the part of a motor which extends inside the cab be it between the front seats or under the front seats. Typical of Class-A rigs, older vans and Class-Cs.

Federal access pass: This discount card lets persons into some federal camp spots for free and allows free entry into many federally controlled points of interest. Retirees, veterans, and disabled persons qualify for the access pass.

Four Wheels Down/4 Wheels on the Ground: This refers to towing a car or light truck by way of a tow bar in which all the toad's wheels are in contact with the pavement while being towed.

Fresh Water Tank: Holds fresh clean potable water for on-board use when a city water hook-up is not available.

Fresh Water Tanks: Most RVs have a fresh water holding tank that provides water when not hooked-up. Tank sizes vary and require regular sanitary cleaning.

Front Toad: The vehicle used to tow a 5th wheel or travel trailer.

Government Campgrounds: Can be county, state, federal/national sites operated by or owned by a government entity. The federal camp providers are listed below. Federal owned campgrounds vary and may provide anything from primitive to full-hook ups camping and ranging in price from free to above the commercial average per night.

Gray Water Tank: On-board storage tank for sink and shower waste water, typically called gray water. Note, it is legal in most places to spill gray water on the ground making outdoor showers legal. Some rigs come with outside showers. Dumping a full gray water tank on the ground is considered bad form and not done. While not as bad as black tank waste, it can still be odoriferous.

GTW: Abbreviation for Gross Trailer Weight.

GVRW (Gross Vehicle Weight Rating): The maximum weight a vehicle can safely carry, including its own weight, passengers, cargo, and any trailer tongue weight. This rating is determined by the vehicle manufacturer and is important for ensuring safe operation and is posted on the vehicle driver's door frame.

Helicoil: Device used to repair a thread striped bolt hole so a bolt can be used in the damaged threaded hole that receives a bolt.

Hook-ups, a noun: This isn't the general term. In RV slang, it means connecting to utilities provided at a campsite that an RV can attach itself to, such as, water, electric power, cable TV or Internet, and sewer. Hooking-up/hook-up, a verb, is the action of attaching a rig to hook-ups. In RV life, it doesn't mean a one-night stand, although some of that goes on as well.

Light Truck Class-C: Usually based on the Toyota light truck from the early '80s into the mid-'90s by various builders such as Dolphin. These small trucks are coveted for good gas mileage and dependability. Good for one person traveling a lot.

Lot Home: Theses are small homes of a bungalow type delivered by truck built on steel frames. They can be but are not necessarily moved once set in place. They are not on foundations but are built like and look like a small house or cabin. They do not typically meet building codes and are not considered to be fixed in place. Often found in RV/ mobile home parks.

Lot Rent: Fee charged to park a rig at an RV/mobile home park.

Mobile Home: Any dwelling that is transported by way of wheels attached to its frame, such as single wide and double wide trailers, park homes, park models, tiny houses, with steel frames. Wheels are often removed. These are often used as permanent homes. Few are ever moved once set in place but they are movable. Classic mobile homes do not have waste tanks.

Modular Home: A house built in two or more pieces and transported to the lot by truck. Once installed, they are not moved but it's not impossible. In the North East they are attached to masonry foundations like any house. In mobile home parks they are often set in place without a foundation on piers or blocks. These are not often seen in mobile home parks.

Motorhome: Is any rig self-powered by its own engine and not towed. They vary from 19 to 32 feet long on average and longer. They can be a Class-C, B, or A rig with various truck chassis.

Park Model: These are generally much like a travel trailer. Unlike a mobile home they are made the same way travel trailers are constructed. They are longer and usually have more slide outs and features like a sliding- glass door or bay window, than a typical camper. They may or may not have waste tanks. They can be moved easily compared to mobile homes and lot homes.

Pickup Truck Camper: These fit inside a full size 8'x4" pickup truck's bed and are removable. Large and heavy models require a 350-size truck. These may come with slide-outs and are surprisingly roomy inside. Most models will have a cab-over bed similar to a Class-C. Lightweight models are for 150 full size bed pickup trucks.

Pop-Rivet Gun: Inexpensive tool used to rivet two metal parts together. Rivets are a two-part compress-together fastener. Rivets are commonly used on everything from blue jeans and Stef bear ear tags to aircraft skins.

Pop-up Camper: Small camper that can be towed by a car or light truck. Pop-ups fold down to a flat configuration for travel and are reassembled or popped up from the trailer's frame by way of struts with a canvas covering. Pop-ups are not hard sided campers with rare exceptions such as the 1960s to 80s Arrow Brand models.

Potable water hose: Usually it is a white or blue like the common garden hoses and is used to provide fresh drinkable (potable) water and provide water for the rig's general use. Potable hose is used to hook-up to a water spigot at a campground or home. Do not use a non-potable hose to provide water for the rig.

Primitive camping: Any campsite or camping place that doesn't provide any amenities.

Private Campgrounds: Owned by individuals or small organizations, usually family owned.

Receiver Hitches: Hitches are devices bolted to a tow vehicle to allow that vehicle the ability to tow. Tow hitches come in a variety of weight capacities and are classed according to that capacity. Class one, two and three hitches are common. A class three hitch is most common and restricted to tow no more than 8,000 GTW and or 800 lbs. of tongue weight. **Warning**: Larger trailers required a greater capacity hitch. Many RVers make the mistake of using an undersized Class-3 hitch for trailers exceeding the weight limit.

Rialta Class-A and B: This is an exception in that they get good gas mileage. Made and imported by Winnebago, they use a Renault engine, are light weight, underpowered, and cleverly designed. Space is limited. Old ones from the 1980s are rare to find but good for extensive travel. Later ones are VW powered. Production stopped in 2005. Good for traveling often.

Rig: This is any camper that is towed or driven and may refer to anything you live in that can be moved legally on public roads. The word rig is interchangeable with the word camper in common speech.

Rube Goldberg: Cartoonist humorist popular in the 1930s into the 1950s who drew crazy, convoluted but complex machines for newspaper's funny pages, machines which performed simple tasks like cracking an egg.

RV Basements: Storage spaces under the interior floor level of an RV accessed from the outside.

RV Generators: Semi-permanent device built into or onto a rig to source 110-volt AC power. The portable versions are typically used on construction sites.

RV Load Center/Panel Box/Distribution Center/Breaker Box: RV load center/panel box/distribution center/breaker box: Like a house breaker box, RV load centers split and allocate incoming power when hooked up into individual circuits with breakers for the 110-V system's power distribution. There will be a main which is a power shut off breaker located inside the panel box. RV load centers have a special feature: Linked to and working with the 110-V system is a power converter which reduces the 110-V power to 12-V power and distributes it from there. 12-volt fuses will be included for the low-voltage system. Smart chargers are also integrated into this arrangement.

RV Sewer Hoses and Fittings: Theses are designed specifically for RV use. Hoses are corrugated and expandable. Fittings for each end are replaceable and designed for RV dumping only. Parts and hoses are easily found at RV stores, some hardware stores, and big box stores such as Walmart.

Safety chains: Use for towing as a backup in case the tongue to ball connection fails. This prevents the tow truck from losing the trailer.

School Bus: Retired school buses are commonly remodeled and converted into a camper by ambitious amateur builders.

Single Wide: These are built on steel frame rails using a mix of regular home and trailer home construction methods. These have regular house utility features and no waste tanks or 12-V systems. Siding is usually vertical aluminum siding and roofs are typically corrugated panel metal roofing. Poorly insulated and flimsy construction is common. They can be up to 60 feet long and 10 to 14 feet wide. Wheels are usually removed once set in place on blocks or piers.

Slide-Out: A slide-out or slide is a section of wall (by way of electric motor) that can be projected outward from the side of an RV to create more interior floor space. When traveling, slide-outs are retracted. Slide-outs are common today and first used beginning it the mid-1980s. Slides add weight and complication to the rig. More stuff that can break although slides rarely malfunction.

Smart Charger: An on-board electrical device designed to maintain RV batteries so that batteries are not overcharged and thus damaged. Unlike older simple chargers, these sense the battery's state and adjust the charge rate as needed to avoid overcharging.

Snowbird: Person who commutes to warmer climates for the cold winter months. These seasonal residents often house in travel trailers/5th wheels. Some own second homes.

Summerbird: Person who travels to cooler climates in the summer to avoid the South's hot weather.

Teardrop Camper: Very small campers only large enough to sleep inside. They are single axle, low ceiling height, and shaped like a teardrop. The kitchen access is typically on the outside behind a rear lift-up body panel. Small cars can usually tow one. Excellent for primitive weekend camping and fast travel. Many people build them. Teardrop camping clubs are common.

Toad: Is any motor vehicle that is towed by the rig, such as a car, and sometimes mounted on the rig's bumper, such as street-legal motorcycle or Moped.

Tongue Stabilizers: A device that is connected from the trailer's tongue to the truck hitch used to aid in balance and tractability by reducing or preventing swaying while towing a trailer. Commonly used on long travel trailers.

Tongue Weight: The amount of weight pressure of the trailer's tongue which should be between 10% and 15% of the trailer's total weight.

Tow Ball: A round steel ball that connects to the truck's hitch to receive the trailer's tongue and link trailer to truck. The balls come in a variety of sizes from 1⅛ diameter to three inches. 2⅛ ball size is common for class three hitches.

Tow bar: A removable device used to hitch a car to the back of a rig to tow the car requiring special brackets on the car.

Toy Hauler: A rig that can carry a motorcycle or off-road vehicle on-board. The rear end, usually a travel trailer or 5th wheel, will fold down and act as a ramp to load the "toy." The toy space often will have fold down beds and other amenities that will allow room to accommodate the recreational vehicle. Only million-dollar buses are known to haul cars this way.

Trailer Tongue: That part of a trailer that extends forward beyond the enclosed living space or cargo space in a V configuration which connects the trailer to the tow vehicle's hitch.

Travel Trailer: These are the classic trailer campers with hard bodies and 1 to 3 axles and often seen towed. They come in sizes from 15' to 40' long x 8' wide. Newer ones have slide-outs except the premium models Airstream and Argosy.

Waste Tanks: On-board RV storage for waste water. Black water tank, or black tank, holds the contents of the toilet. Gray water, or gray tank, holds waste water from sinks and showers.

Water Pressure Reducer: This device fits on a potable water hose spigots to reduce incoming high-pressure water from the hook-up source.

Wheel Chock or Chock: A block wedged behind or in front of a wheel on the ground used to prevent a trailer or motor vehicle from rolling. Once a trailer is detached from a tow vehicle which acts as a brake and or control the trailer's brakes, nothing stops that trailer from rolling. Warning: Always chock a detached trailer. Chocks can be purchased or made. A brick, lumber cutoff or a stone will work in a pitch.

Work-camper: A person who travels for work and temporarily lives in RV parks near their work.

ABOUT THE AUTHORS

Rachel Thompson, former freelance writer, wrote and cartooned for magazines and newspapers from the Lehigh Valley, Pa. before taking up the motorhome life. She now resides deep inside a national forest in Florida. She became a serious writer after first surviving a near death motor vehicle accident in 2003 after more than 25 years in the construction industry. To date, she has self-published six novels and two collections of short stories available in print and e-book. Her quirky and satirical short stories have appeared in a variety of anthologies. The next novel is in process now. Nonfiction credits include press releases, ad-copy and other materials for nonprofit organizations. From sci-fi and fantasy, to social satire and historical fiction, Thompson twists it all.

Rachel's Email: humanrights4all@aol.com.
RCThom.com or RCThom.net for her website with info about her books.

Lisa Cross taught drafting & architecture in industrial arts programs for a number of years before going into industry where she held a variety of positions related to mechanical engineering, industrial equipment maintenance, and supervision. She also taught the construction trades and later briefly worked in the construction industry as a field manager and job coordinator. She was known for her expertise, attention to details, and problem-solving skills in several mechanical fields. Her willingness to dig deep and get her hands dirty made her an asset. Today she is retired, and currently spends her time cooking, baking bread and various styles of pizza, and enjoying nature and her musical interests.

Index

Books by Rachel C. Thompson
Available in print and e-book

Soul Harvest:
Print ISBN number: 798-1-7321459-1-7   E-book: 798-1-7321459-0-0
Aggie in Orbit:
Print ISBN number: 798-1-7321459-7-9   E-book: 798-1-7321459-6-2
Aggie in Space:
Print ISBN number: 798-1-7321459-8-6   E-book: 798-1-7321459-9-3
Dragon Fire:
Print ISBN number: 798-1-7321459-2-4   E-book: 798-1-7321459-3-1
Stalking Kilgore Trout:
Print ISBN number: 798-1-7321459-4-8   E-book: 798-1-7321459-5-5
Book of Answers:
Print ISBN number: 979-8-9861808-0-9   E-book: 979-8-9861808-1-6
Another Anthology:
Print ISBN number: 979-8-9861808-2-3   E-book 979-8-9861808-3-0
The Adventures of Tom Conley
Print ISBN 979-8-9861808-4-7
Ebook ISBN 979-8-9861808-7-8 (International)

Amazon only three satirical short stories in each three pack for $1.99
        President's Three Pack
        GLBT 3 Pack
        Heretic's 3 Pack

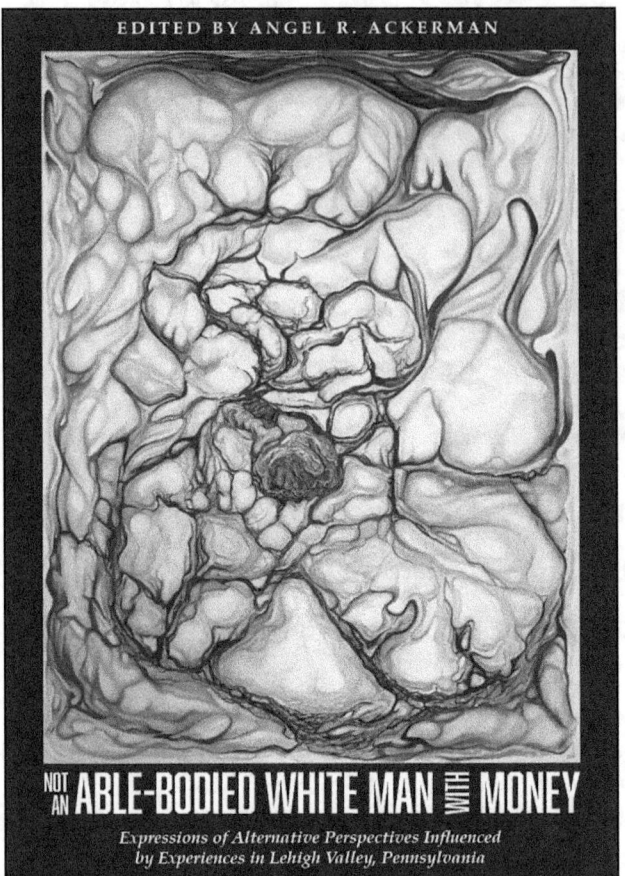

Interested in more personal experiences including Rachel?

Not an Able-Bodied
White Man with Money:
Expressions of Alternative Perspectives Influenced
by Experiences in Lehigh Valley, Pennsylvania

Edited by Angel R. Ackerman

This volume explores various non-fiction voices associated with the Lehigh Valley. It tackles experiences of sexual/gender non-heteronormativity, disability, neurodivergence, mental health, body image, ethnic minorities, & more.

Other personal experience nonfiction from Parisian Phoenix Publishing:

Stops Along The Way
By Charles Ticho

Toward the end of his life, nonagenarian Charles Ticho compiled this book of essays about his childhood as a Jew escaping the Holocaust during World War II. Thanks to his youth at the time, and his American mother, he relocated to the United States. This book chronicles his family's experience during the war, told from the innocent perspective of a child. We also see the family rebuild from nothing and follow Ticho's career in film production.

The Phulasso Devotional
Engineering the Warrior Priest for Dark Times
By Thurston D. Gill Jr.

Gill presents his approach to keeping your loved ones safe in an increasingly violent world in this devotional, *The Phulasso Devotional: Engineering the Warrior Priest for Dark Times*, based in Biblical texts, but designed for all people who want to maintain their spiritual values when faced with hard choices.

TWISTS: Gathered Ephemera
By darrell parry

An eclectic collection of poems is now in its second edition, including a poem previously unreleased. Parry's quirky wisdom delivers messages that might make the reader laugh or cry.

The Emotionally Intelligent Dental Office
By Steven Hymovitch, DDS, MBA, CEC

Dr. Stephen Hymovitch offers practical advice from the trenches of his dental office. In this fun volume, Dr. H combines tales of personal experience with business advice from his expertise in emotional intelligence and leadership to create a book that will help you deal with unruly clients, be a good boss, and work with different personality types among other practical lessons.

PARISIAN PHOENIX
PUBLISHING

DO YOU WANT TO HELP PARISIAN PHOENIX OR ANY SMALL PUBLISHER OR INDEPENDENT AUTHOR?

- Buy books. Buy more books. Give books as gifts.
- Recommend authors to friends.
- Share Social Media Posts.
- Leave a review:
  Amazon
  Goodreads
  Google Books

  Learn how

  - Readers use reviews to find books.
  - Retailers' web sites use reviews as part of their algorithm.
  - Some advertisers require a certain number of reviews.
- Join and share newsletters.
- Attend events.
- Join Goodreads and follow authors, mark their books as read, shelve and rate them.
- Check on Patreon and Kickstarter for the creators you love
- Start a book club.

Subscribe to our Newsletter, "Bookish Babble", on

substack

https://parisianphoenixpublishing.substack.com/

www.ingramcontent.com/pod-product-compliance
Lightning Source LLC
Chambersburg PA
CBHW070959120626
46546CB00004B/1698